What Pe

...

"Charles Whitfield's book, *My Recovery: A Personal Plan for Healing,* is a major and important contribution to the recovery literature. It is a must-read for anyone who is serious about recovery from addiction, mental health problems or chronic lifestyle-related illness. This book is written in an easy-to-understand style without losing a clear and insightful focus on the critical areas of the recovery process. It's a book to keep near your bedside so the key ideas can be read, reviewed and reflected upon."

Terence T. Gorski
author and president of The CENAPS Corporation,
Spring Hill, Florida

"To know what 'recovery' is all about—read this book. If you are 1) In recovery, 2) a therapist or psychiatrist, 3) or a treatment program administrator, it is a MUST-read! It gives a DETAILED MAP with specific directions! Dr. Whitfield weaves the therapy process and the Twelve Steps into a magnificent plan for recovery. This should be a standard textbook for treatment programs worldwide. I use it with our staff and patients. It lays out the path for authentic healing. A major contribution!"

Jim Corrington Jr., MSW, CISW
Addiction Treatment Services
Banner Behavioral Health, Scottsdale, Arizona

My RECOVERY

A PERSONAL PLAN FOR HEALING

CHARLES L. WHITFIELD, M.D.

Author of the bestselling *Healing the Child Within,*
A Gift to Myself and *Co-Dependence*

Health Communications, Inc.
Deerfield Beach, Florida

www.bcibooks.com

Library of Congress Cataloging-in-Publication Data

Whitfield, Charles L.
    My recovery : a personal plan for healing / Charles L. Whitfield.
        p.   cm.
    Includes bibliographical references.
    ISBN 0-7573-0120-7 (tp)
    1. Psychotherapist and patient. 2. Psychotherapy. I. Title.

RC480.8 W495 2003
616.89'14–dc22

                                                                    2003056552

©2003 Charles L. Whitfield
ISBN 0-0753-0120-7

All rights reserved. Printed in the United States of America. No part of this publication may be reproduced, stored in a retrieval system or transmitted in any form or by any means, electronic, mechanical, photocopying, recording or otherwise, without the written permission of the publisher.

HCI, its Logos and Marks are trademarks of Health Communications, Inc.

Publisher: Health Communications, Inc.
                3201 S.W. 15th Street
                Deerfield Beach, FL 33442-8190

Cover design by Peter Quintal
Inside book design by Dawn Von Strolley Grove

CONTENTS

Contents

Contents

STATEMENT OF INTENT

While potentially helpful and personally empowering for healing, this book is intended to supplement and strengthen a full recovery program that is specific to whatever problem, condition or disorder a person may have. It uses and expands the principles of treatment and recovery planning.

This book is not intended to replace the counsel of a licensed clinician or therapist in sorting out individual concerns and healing from these problems and disorders. Each person's case is unique and deserves special attention. This book will likely work best when used in combination with seeing a recovery-savvy clinician regularly and using other recovery aids as appropriate.

The attached references may assist the reader with the further exploration and explanation of this important information. For a more complete account of the link between mental disorders and childhood and other trauma, the reader may refer to my two companion books, *The Truth about Depression* and *The Truth about Mental Illness*. To supplement using this current volume, the reader may also wish to look at *A Gift to Myself*, which is a workbook and guide to help in the healing process for Stage Two recovery.

ACKNOWLEDGMENTS

A special acknowledgment and thanks to Barbara Whitfield for her assistance and enthusiasm in completing this book. Also to those who have contributed in diverse and important ways. These include: Jim Corrington, Terence Gorski, Earl Harrison, C.A. Killoran, Robynne Moran, Sally Merchant, Karen R. Jones, Mary Jackson, Lorna Hecker, Peter Vegso, Christine Belleris, Allison Janse, Kathy Grant, Kim Weiss, Paola Fernandez, Elisabeth Rinaldi, Suzanne Smith and all of the fine staff at Health Communications. A special thanks to Tennessee Dixon for permission to print her watercolor Unfinished Business.

Also great appreciation to the founders and countless members of Twelve-Step fellowships.

A special thanks to all of my patients for their courageous work that over the years inspired me to formulate the information you are about to read.

INTRODUCTION

This is a simple book.

It demystifies the process of healing.

It makes recovery easier by adding clarity, structure, and most important, it supports using your own personal power as a major recovery aid.

Do conventional treatments for illness work? For most acute diseases or conditions—from sore throats to broken bones—the answer is "yes."

But for most chronic diseases, the answer is that most conventional treatments don't work well. They are not always effective. A reason for this is that these standard treatments usually relieve only the symptoms. They don't address the actual or deeper causes. And they don't tend to use all of the various options or aids for recovery.

Most chronic illnesses are multidimensional in their origin and how they affect our lives. They have physical, mental, emotional and spiritual layers or aspects. To heal most successfully we need to address each of these dimensions, one by one, which I describe in some detail in this book.

I originally wrote these three recovery plan guides to help my own patients recover from addictions, depression, posttraumatic stress disorder and other illnesses. I have added the other explanatory chapters, most of which are previously unpublished, to supplement the original recovery guides. These are in the form of reader-friendly interviews.

Using the material in this book will likely help people with chronic illness heal faster. If they apply their personal goals and methods, and work their recovery plan with patience and persistence, it will make their healing flow with more clarity and success.

Charles L. Whitfield, M.D.
Atlanta, Georgia
August, 2003

1

Introduction to the Stages of Recovery

An Interview with
Charles L. Whitfield, M.D.
by Barbara Whitfield, R.T., C.M.T

In this chapter, Barbara Whitfield interviews Charles Whitfield about the origins of his ideas and work using these recovery plans. Dr. Whitfield shows how doing so can be personally empowering, and then discusses the role of using spirituality in the process of healing.

Origins

Barbara Whitfield: Even today, books on conventional medicine, psychiatry and psychology don't mention *stages* of recovery from any illness or problem. How did you discover these stages? And how useful are they?

Charles Whitfield: I came upon them when I watched, over time, how my patients recovered. I discovered them slowly, over a twelve-year span from about 1973 through 1985. At first I observed people with alcoholism and other drug dependence as they were recovering. I noticed a number of things about them, including how effective early intervention and treatment could be, but at the same time, how commonly they relapsed. Many could stay abstinent from drugs and alcohol for a long time, only to relapse months or years later. I asked myself, "Why?"

Most of their relapses usually turned out to be due to a *low participation* in a recovery program, or to their *unhealed painful effects of trauma*—or both. I began to see how this early struggle for a successful abstinence from alcohol and other drugs was only the beginning of healing for many of them.

In the mid 1980s, I saw that identifying and expressing their pain that was left over from childhood and later trauma helped a lot of these people. It freed them from most of their stored toxic energy enough so that their relapses lessened or stopped, and they started to feel and function better. So here were the first two of the stages of recovery, Stages One and Two, unfolding in my patients. These included getting an early recovery started and stabilized (Stage One), and then if they chose, working at a deeper level of healing on the almost universal finding of having bothersome effects of childhood and other trauma (Stage Two). I outline these in Table 1, which reads from the bottom up.

Table 1. Recovery & Duration According to Stages

Recovery Stage	Condition	Focus of Recovery	Approximate Duration
3	Human/ spiritual	Spirituality	Ongoing
2	Trauma effects	Trauma-specific full recovery program	3 to 5 years
1	Stage Zero disorder	Basic-illness specific full recovery program	½ to 3 years
0	Active illness	Addiction, compulsion or disorder	Indefinite
		-------------------	
		Woundedness, trauma effects	

Q: Did these observations change the way you practiced as a physician?

A: Yes, they did. Because I saw that this stage-oriented approach worked well for many of my patients, I told others about using this kind of approach as an option among their healing choices, too. And among those who used it, most of them got better. So this approach in stages was and continues to be empowering. It gives the individual more personal power. It also names and breaks down the various parts of the recovery process, so that it is not so imposing or overwhelming.

The first stage was to stabilize their illness, in these earlier cases, alcoholism or other chemical dependence. Then, if they had a history of childhood trauma—which it turns out most of them did—and if they wanted to heal from the effects of that trauma, they could do some deeper healing work around that.

This sequence was not new. Some clinicians had used it already, even though it was not clearly described in the clinical textbooks or journals. But what I did that was new was to refine and describe the *structure of the core issues* and the *recovery tasks* within each of these two stages. I then wrote it all out in a reader-friendly format so that my patients would have a clearer way to see and understand their recovery tasks and process.

PERSONAL POWER

Q: Did you do anything else that was different?

A: I did. One thing that I've always found most helpful with patients is to involve them as much as possible in the process of planning their treatment. I knew that using a formal *treatment plan* and process was a state requirement for any licensed addiction treatment facility. But it was the *clinician* who had to write the treatment plan, not the patient. I thought that took away some of the patient's personal power and made it less likely for the patient to own it and follow its actions.

So I simply added a clear explanation of how to write one's *own recovery plan*. This used the same format as formal treatment planning, which I had simplified for them in these guides. I added that to the reader-friendly educational material that I had already outlined in writing for them. I've refined it over the years, and that time-tested and proven version for each of the recovery stages is what the reader now has in this book. Using such an individualized recovery plan is empowering for people. It gives them more *personal power* and *motivation* for their recovery.

Q: How about core recovery issues? Does addressing them help?

A: It does. Core recovery issues help in all three of these stages. I list and discuss them in each of the guidelines. Naming and then working through each of them as they come up for us gives us a great healing advantage. Doing that gives us still more personal power.

Spirituality

Q: We know that spirituality is an important component in recovery from addiction It helps the whole process work better. How did you incorporate it into all this as a third stage, i.e., as Stage Three?

A: By the late 1980s, I had written the first draft of *My Recovery Plan* for Stages One and Two. I had also already been talking about spirituality regularly with my patients. We knew that there was really not a separate stage that separated spirituality from the first two stages. Spirituality was important and useful *all the way*—throughout the entire recovery process.

But I noticed that many of my patients had a hard time with the spiritual stuff. For various reasons, a lot of them had been hurt by some of their experiences with organized religion. That, combined with their having been abused by their parents and sometimes their teachers, had often left them with a big issue of not being able to trust authority figures. It is no wonder that they then had a hard time knowing and trusting perhaps our ultimate authority—God.

I also saw that a lot of my patients *did* eventually find a nourishing spirituality with and from their Higher Power or God, *after* they were well progressed in their Stage Two work. I believe that the main reason for this is because by that time in their recovery they knew their *real self*, which I also call the "Child Within." By knowing their Child Within they were free to experientially connect to God more easily. Our false self can't know God authentically.

After finishing this Stage Two work, more of them had a kind of hunger for the spiritual. They wanted more spiritual nourishment. Because of this, I wrote out a third and final component of *My Recovery* and called it "Stage Three." I did that even though I knew that the whole journey was and is spiritual. Even in Stage Zero, when we have not yet started recovery, we are still spiritual seekers, although we may not know that yet, as Carl Jung implied when he wrote to AA co-founder Bill Wilson in the 1930s.

On our life's journey, we are in one way or another asking ourselves those perennial questions: *Who am I? What am I doing here?* and *Where am I going?* A related question is *How can I get any peace?*

Q: With the importance and usefulness of AA in Stage One work, how do AA's Twelve Steps fit into this whole process?

A: They are clearly useful from the start. And they continue to be psychologically and spiritually nourishing throughout recovery Stages One and Two. So they fit in appropriately and practically. That is why I have included and emphasized them in the structure of these first two Stage plans in this book. Because of their importance, I have also included the entire transcript of the interview that we did on the Twelve Steps in this book, as well (see chapters 5 through 9, starting on page 65).

Q: What about Stage Two recovery? How does it fit in here? Can you say more about that?

A: Yes. Stage Two fits in as a crucial part of the whole process of recovery. I also include an interview that I did with Dr. Lorna Hecker, in which I describe some of the important features of Stage Two recovery work, in chapter 3 (starting on page 29).

Q: Which chapter is the most important for readers to look at first? Should they start with a particular one of these three interviews? Or should they read the material in each recovery plan first?

A: I don't think it matters where a person starts. Reading any one of these first prepares us for reading another. I do recommend that people focus on the section that addresses their particular sequence in their own recovery, right now. For example, if you are just beginning recovery from any illness now, then I suggest that you focus your reading on the Stage One material. If you have finished most of your Stage One work—i.e., your original illness or problem is well stabilized for at least a few months, or preferably a year or more (unless you've been relapsing)—then you might consider looking at the Stage Two material. The questions and answers on the

Twelve Steps (chapters 5 through 9) can be read almost any-time during any of the recovery stages.

Q: What about using this stage-oriented approach to heal-ing from other illnesses? Are addictions the only ones for which they are useful?

A: After using them with patients—who had various prob-lems and illnesses—for more than fifteen years now, I believe that these stages are mostly generic in their application. They are useful in healing from depression, anxiety problems and most of the other psychological disorders. They can also be useful in helping to heal from some physical illness, if child-hood trauma is in the history and/or if the person is a spiri-tual seeker.

Q: So if someone has migraine headaches and is being treated by a physician in a Stage One fashion, Stage Two work could address the pain on a deeper level if there is a his-tory of trauma. Is that right?

A: Yes. I also describe some of the documented links between physical illness and childhood trauma in *The Truth about Mental Illness.*

2

My Recovery Plan for Stage One Recovery:

Basic Healing from Addictions, Compulsions and Other Disorders

GETTING STARTED

To get somewhere, it's useful to know where you are going.

No matter what condition, concern or problem you might be recovering from, you might already have some idea about what you want to happen—where you want to go—regarding that condition.

To accomplish what you want to happen in your recovery and in your life, it can be useful to make a Recovery Plan. (In a treatment facility or program, this may also be called a "treatment plan.")

In making this plan, you can start by giving a name to what condition or conditions you might have. These conditions may fall under any of the following categories:

- Any addiction
- Any compulsion
- Unhealthy attachment
- Any physical illness
- Any mental illness
- Any other condition

These conditions may be acute, recurring or chronic. Can you in any way identify with having one or more of these? In the space below, write any responses to this question that might come up for you. Talk to your therapist or counselor if you have any questions.

_____

_____

_____

_____

_____

_____

Naming any Conditions

Depending on their nature, these conditions might:

• Heal spontaneously
• Require specific intervention
• Linger on for a long time, even for a lifetime.

What is so hopeful about identifying any of them is that there is a way out of their confusion, pain and suffering. Recovery is possible. And with a participation in a full recovery program, recovery is likely.

I list some brief definitions of several of these conditions below. For questions regarding any of these, ask your therapist or counselor.

Chemical Dependence (including alcoholism)—Recurring trouble associated with drinking or using other drugs. The trouble may be in any one or more of several life areas: physical, mental, emotional, spiritual and relationships (including family), job, legal or financial.

Compulsive Gambling—Recurring trouble associated with betting, gambling, investing or financially risking in any way. The trouble may be in any of the areas listed under chemical dependence above.

Compulsive Spending—Recurring trouble associated with spending money for any reason, whether associated with shopping, impulsive buying, using credit cards or any other way of spending.

Eating Disorder—A recurring pattern of any one or a combination of overeating, bingeing, purging, not eating or overeating with dieting or compulsive exercising, usually used unconsciously to avoid authentic relationship with self, others or Higher Power (or God or whatever name you choose).

Sexual Addiction—Sexual activity of any kind, including repeated fantasizing, that recurringly interferes with or substitutes for our relationship with ourselves or with others, including our spouse.

Incest or Sexual Abuse—Any inappropriate talking, flirting, touching or fondling, or any other sexual activity with any family member or step-members or any other child. It is usually done by a person who is one-up or in a position of power to a person who is one-down or vulnerable.

Verbal Abuse—Any demeaning, shaming, judging or putting-down used to avoid authentic relationships with self or others. May escalate to rageaholism.

Rageaholism (Verbal Violence)—Recurring use of fits of anger, rage, screaming or yelling to control, manipulate or avoid authentic relationships with self and others.

Violence or Physical Abuse—Physical lashing out or attacking of any kind, usually with the intent, whether conscious or unconscious, to control or harm another.

Workaholism—Working to the detriment of our relationship with ourselves or with others, especially family or other close people.

Religious Addiction—A recurring pattern of using religion in any one or a combination of ways: judgmentalism, self-righteousness, rigidity, or as a way to alter one's state of consciousness, usually used unconsciously to avoid our authentic relationship with self, others or Higher Power.

Nicotine Addiction—Recurring use of nicotine in any form, whether as tobacco or the chronic use of Nicoret gum. A form of chemical dependence.

Mental Illness—Any mental or emotional disorder whether associated with recurring fears, sadness, emptiness, harmful behaviors or any other dysfunction, and whether or not the person ever recovered or received treatment for it. May be mistaken for or associated with any of the above conditions. Commonly trauma related.

Physical Illness—Any physical condition or illness.

Co-dependence—Suffering and dysfunction associated with or due to focusing on the needs or behavior of others. Usually underlies, contributes to or aggravates most of the above conditions.

Can you identify in any way with any of these?

To understand better the process of recovery, we can say that anyone who has any of the above conditions in an active way is in Stage Zero recovery. They are not yet in recovery.

Until a person begins recovery, they will usually remain in Stage Zero—the active illness or condition—with all of its suffering and consequences. Unless they heal spontaneously, as may happen with some physical illnesses, it is probable that without a recovery program the illness or condition will continue for many years, if not last for an entire lifetime, depending on the condition and its causes.

RECOVERY

Recovery offers a gradually increasing freedom from the suffering and other consequences of the illness or condition.

The first step in recovery is to identify and name any illness or condition that we may have. In the space below, if you choose, write the name(s) of any condition(s) that you might in any way identify with having.

_____

_____

_____

_____

_____

Once we have identified and named the illness or condition, we have started our recovery. We are beginning what some call Stage One recovery.

Given that I have this Stage Zero condition, what now do I want to happen? A person may answer "I want to make a successful recovery from _____."

(fill in the blank)

However you may answer that question, *you have begun your recovery plan.* If you choose, write your answer to the question "What do I want to happen?" in the space below.

_____

_____

_____

_____

_____

_____

You are now two-thirds of the way through completing the first draft of your recovery plan. To complete it, consider your answer to a second question: "Given what I want to happen, specifically how can I accomplish what I want to happen?"

This may be more difficult to answer. Feel free to ask your therapist, counselor or therapy group for help with this one and take plenty of time. Use the space below to write your answer.

_____

_____

_____

_____

_____

_____

THE RECOVERY PLAN FOR STAGE ONE

Having written the above, you are now ready to write out a formal recovery plan. To assist you in this process, I have written some sample plans on the following pages. You may borrow from any of them or use your own ideas, as well as any suggestions from others that may be helpful.

Problem or Condition	What I Want to Happen (Goals)	How I Plan to Reach These Goals
Chemical dependence	Make a successful recovery.	1. Abstain from alcohol and other mood-changing drugs, one day at a time.
	Live free of chemicals, one day at a time.	2. Change myself from within.
	Begin to change from within.	a. Attend_____ 12-Step meetings each week.
		b. Work the program with a sponsor—whom I will identify by _____ (date).
		c. Attend group therapy each week at _____ for _____ (duration).
		d. Attend CD education at _____ for _____ (number of sessions).

(continued on next page)

15

My Recovery

Problem or Condition	What I Want to Happen (Goals)	How I Plan to Reach These Goals
Eating disorder	Make a successful recovery.	1. Abstain from foods and habits of eating that are detrimental to my recovery.
	Develop and maintain a healthy relationship with food, eating and myself.	2. Change myself from within. a. Attend _____ Overeaters Anonymous meetings each week. b. Work the program with a sponsor—whom I will identify by _____ (date). c. Attend group (and/or individual) therapy each week at _____ for _____ (duration).

MY RECOVERY PLAN

Name (optional) _____ Date _____

Problem or Condition	What I Want to Happen (Goals)	How I Plan to Reach These Goals

CORE RECOVERY ISSUES FOR STAGE ONE

In making your first recovery plan and in making regular updates of the plan later on, you might find it useful to consider any of a number of core issues in early recovery.

An *issue* is any conflict, concern or potential problem, whether conscious or unconscious, that is incomplete for us—or needs action or change. A core issue is one that comes up repeatedly for many people in their recovery.

These core issues tend to come up in (1) **recovery** itself, (2) **relationships,** (3) **problems in living,** (4) day-to-day **conflicts** and (5) any so-called **"character defects,"** as addressed by the Fourth and the Fifth of the Twelve Steps.

In *early* recovery these core issues may include:

- Abstinence
- Self-discipline
- Self-monitoring
- Overcoming isolation
- Repairing and rebuilding relationships
- Accepting responsibility for self
- Leisure time
- Denial
- Grieving losses
- Tolerating feelings
- Sex
- Avoiding people with active Stage Zero conditions
- Identity and self-esteem
- Control
- Having fun

INTEGRATING CORE ISSUES INTO YOUR RECOVERY PLAN

Based on your own individual recovery wants and needs, it can be helpful to address any of these core issues in your recovery plan.

Look over the preceding list or Table 2 (pages 20 and 21) of core issues and consider which of these may be of special concern to you in your recovery.

Then, for each one that you choose, ask yourself the same two questions: "What do I want to happen regarding this issue or area of my life?" and "Given what I want to happen, specifically how can I accomplish that?"

Some people simply don't know yet how to accomplish their goals. Just identifying goals may be enough at first. You may need to explore with your therapist and/or in your therapy group how to accomplish what you want to happen. Give yourself time to do this. Make this commitment to yourself as soon as you can. *Don't worry* about making or doing it "PERFECT." Remember that this is just the beginning, and you can revise your plan as you go along.

In your first plan, keep it simple. While all these core issues may be important for you in some way, don't feel as if you have to use many of them. For your first plan, you may wish to pick only the two or three issues that are of most concern to you. As an example, I have selected three core issues and written a possible recovery plan on page 22.

Core Issues in Stage One Recovery*

Issues	Early	Middle	Advanced Recovery
1. Abstinence.	Maintaining alcohol and drug-free** status; keeping it simple.	Ongoing, one day at a time.	Ongoing.
2. Self-discipline.	Setting limits on self; keeping to details of recovery program.	Ongoing.	Ongoing.
3. Self-monitoring.	Realizing we have needs. Accepting feedback from others to make transition to identifying for ourself.	Identifying needs; recognize physical, emotional, spiritual signals that say something needs attention.	Self-monitoring and getting needs met.
4. Overcoming isolation. Re-learning how to be with people comfortably without drugs.	Recognizing, tolerating and dealing with social fears.	Taking action. Building social network.	Ongoing.
5. Repairing/ rebuilding relationships, especially close friendships and family.	Identification and assessment of current relationships.	Making amends, healthier choices. Re-establishing relationships.	Adult Child and Co-dependence recovery.
6. Accepting responsibility for self.	Awareness through self-examination and feedback from others.	Owning problems, taking responsibility. Stop blaming. Getting out of victim role.	Empowering.
7. Denial.	Denial of addiction, disease; accepting seriousness of it.	Acceptance and dealing with denial as a response to life situations.	Ongoing.
8. Leisure time.	Managing unstructured time; getting through without drugs.**	Increasing quantity and quality of activities designed to enhance self.	Ongoing.

Issues	Early	Middle	Advanced Recovery
9. **Having fun.**	Learning how to redefine and experience fun without using alcohol or other drugs.**	Ongoing.	Ongoing.
10. **Grieving.**	Identifying our losses, especially the addiction, the high, the lifestyle and the identity.	Learning and beginning to grieve. Later, letting go of what we have lost.	Adult Child and Co-dependence recovery (healing the Child Within).
11. **Tolerating feelings.**	Recognizing and identifying (especially fear, anger, shame and joy).	Experiencing feelings and working through them.	Experiencing, observing and using our feelings.
12. **Sex.**	Awareness of the impairment of sexual life as a result of condition.	Developing a healthy sexuality.	Ongoing.
13. **Closing doors on drug-oriented peers and lifestyles.**	Doing it.	Keeping them closed, learning how to be selective.	Ongoing.
14. **Identity, self-image, self-esteem.**	Awareness of low self-esteem, damaged self-image.	Tolerating feelings, learning how to forgive self. Discovering who I am without drugs, etc.	Adult Child and Co-dependence recovery (healing the Child Within).
15. **Control.**	Accepting powerlessness, learning what I don't have control of, awareness of where locus of control lies; developing and using the ability to change what I can.	Ongoing.	Ongoing.

*Modified from Jones & Merchant, 1986.
For other conditions, substitute appropriate **substance, behavior or **relationships**.

21

MY RECOVERY PLAN—EXAMPLE USING THREE CORE RECOVERY ISSUES

Problem or Condition	What I Want to Happen (Goals)	How I Plan to Reach These Goals
Isolation	Stop being so isolated.	1. Attend _____ Twelve-Step meetings each week.
		2. Call a friend three times a week.
		3. Attend weekly group therapy.
		4. Meet or go out with a friend once a week.
Denial	See my reality for what it is.	1. Begin to examine how I see things in my life and how I feel about them.
		2. Notice any craving that I might experience.
		3. Share this with my Twelve-Step or therapy group weekly.
		4. Ask for feedback from safe people.

Problem or Condition	What I Want to Happen (Goals)	How I Plan to Reach These Goals
Difficulty recognizing and tolerating my feelings	Begin to learn to recognize and tolerate my feelings.	1. If I feel "bad," notice that and share the details of how that feels with a safe person and/or write it in my journal. 2. If I feel "good," notice that and share the details of how that feels with a safe person and/or write it in my journal. 3. Share at least one specific feeling (e.g., fear, anger, shame, joy) with a safe person each day. 4. When a "bad" feeling comes up, just be with it, share about it with a safe person. (It won't last forever!)

When you make your first recovery plan, you may be in either an inpatient or an outpatient setting.*

As you progress in your recovery, you can make it go better if you will (1) place a copy of your recovery plan in a prominent place where you can see it every day (caution: don't leave it for toxic people to read), (2) read it over carefully every week, and (3) every few months, review it based on how your recovery is progressing, making any changes you might consider useful. (You can ask your therapist, counselor, sponsor and therapy group for suggestions here.)

DEVELOPING A STABLE AND SOLID RECOVERY

It usually takes a while to develop a stable recovery in a Stage One program. Give yourself plenty of time.

If it is your first time in recovery, take at least one year—or longer—in a Stage One full recovery program before you consider moving into Stage Two recovery.

RELAPSE

If you have relapsed after your first plan, you might want to consider beginning some Stage Two recovery work, concomitant with a Stage One full recovery program. (Ask your therapist or counselor for suggestions about this.)

Repeated relapsing usually means that one or both of two possible problems may be present:

---

*Some may use this recovery plan and not be in any kind of formal therapy. If so, and if you have any difficulty with your recovery or if you simply want some assistance in your recovery, I suggest that you see a therapist or counselor with expertise in your area of recovery for a consultation.

1. Your recovery plan, and possibly your participation in it, *may need to be strengthened.*
2. Your relapsing may be due to *unresolved Stage Two "Adult Child" (i.e., childhood trauma) recovery issues.*

Ask your therapist or counselor for assistance in addressing and handling these problems.

You may also wish to make a relapse prevention plan as either part of or separate from your basic Stage One recovery plan. There are some books available with guidelines for relapse prevention planning. Ask your counselor for details.

In addition to making a relapse prevention plan, a great help in relapse prevention is to work each of the Twelve Steps, one by one, slowly and with a sponsor. It is preferable that your sponsor also has formerly and similarly worked whichever step you currently plan to work. To work the Twelve Steps in a healing way usually takes several years, and it may be appropriate to re-work any and all of the steps later.

STAGE TWO RECOVERY

Once you have a stable and solid Stage One recovery—one that has lasted for at least one year* or longer—it may be time to consider looking into your Adult Child (i.e., childhood trauma) issues. One major manifestation of these trauma effects is co-dependence, which I define on page 12. While these trauma effects do not cause Stage Zero conditions, they do regularly aggravate them and thus contribute to relapse.

Underlying most of the Stage One conditions is a wounding, which I describe in *Healing the Child Within; A Gift to*

---

*This duration is for some conditions, such as alcoholism and other chemical dependence. For other conditions, such as an eating disorder or workaholism, this duration may be shortened. However, no matter when a person chooses to begin Stage Two recovery, an ongoing Stage One recovery program will strengthen Stage Two recovery.

Myself; Co-Dependence; Boundaries and Relationships; Memory and Abuse; The Truth about Depression, and *The Truth about Mental Illness.* Rather than feeling as if we are bad, sick, crazy or stupid, we discover that we are none of these. Rather, we were and still are simply wounded. Our response to this wounding was not abnormal. It was actually an adaptive and normal reaction to the overly stressful situation of growing up in an unhealthy, troubled or dysfunctional family, and perhaps continuing to be stressed or traumatized into our adolescent and adult lives. This normal reaction was both taught to us and learned by us. And *what is learned can be unlearned.*

I describe the full recovery program for the Adult Child condition and co-dependence in the next Recovery Plan section, My Recovery Plan for Stage Two Recovery (chapter 4) and in more detail in *A Gift to Myself* and *Co-Dependence.*

STAGE THREE RECOVERY

Stage Three recovery is spirituality. You might have already begun to incorporate it into your life. I describe this further in My Recovery Plan for Stage Three Recovery.

Whenever you feel ready to begin working in Stages Two and Three recovery, you can look into making a recovery plan for these. Ask your therapist, counselor and therapy group for their feedback if you want to begin these.

I wish you the best on your journey and in your adventure of recovery.

MY RECOVERY PLAN

Name (optional) _____   Date _____

Problem or Condition	What I Want to Happen (Goals)	How I Plan to Reach These Goals

MY RECOVERY PLAN

Name (optional) _____ Date _____

Problem or Condition	What I Want to Happen (Goals)	How I Plan to Reach These Goals

3

Introduction to Stage Two Recovery

AN INTERVIEW WITH CHARLES WHITFIELD BY LORNA HECKER, PH.D.

"As clinicians we are sometimes too often in a hurry to make the patient's pain go away, when in fact the *pain* itself *may be a learning tool.*"

In this chapter Lorna Hecker interviews Charles Whitfield about his clinical experience and research in the treatment of adult survivors of childhood trauma. Here he continues to discuss the stages of recovery in general and Stage Two in particular. He gives clinical advice on the treatment of abuse-related trauma effects and describes some recent research results. This chapter is a new and expanded version of an article published in a useful but sometimes hard to find journal [Hecker, Lorna L., Whitfield, Charles L. "Advice and Adage: Interview with Charles L. Whitfield, M.D., on the Psychotherapy of Childhood Trauma Survivors," *Journal of Clinical Activities, Assignments & Handouts in Psychotherapy Practice* I.3 (2000): 95–103].

Lorna Hecker: I know that looking at a history of trauma is important in recovery for many people. What are some of the ways that trauma can affect a person?

Charles Whitfield: The effects of trauma are many and varied. They can affect any of several of our crucial life areas in the way we function. Trauma changes a normal, healthy life into a more difficult one. At the same time, there's no one disorder or group of symptoms that are diagnostic of trauma, although there are many that are strongly suggestive, such as the presence of an addiction or recurring depressions or dissociative identity disorder. I think that showing a table from page 200 of my book *The Truth about Depression* may be helpful to clarify the broad and vast ways that trauma can affect us. I include a copy of this table here labeled Potential Results of Unresolved Trauma.

While this table presents just a brief overview, it may serve to describe some of these general life areas and ways that trauma can affect us. Probably the most useful thing to do with this table is to read it over and see if there are any ways that a person can identify. If there are, this can be the beginning of healing, since when we *name things accurately* it can give us personal power, depending what we do with that naming.

If we then *link* these symptoms, life difficulties or effects *with the trauma* and then *grieve* our losses in the company of safe people, over time we can slowly heal.

This process usually unfolds most successfully when we do it in the context of a full recovery program that we ourselves plan. This is why I wrote these guides for each of the stages of recovery.

Q: What advice would you give people who are starting to do Stage Two recovery work?

A: People can determine their own personal recovery goals. The goals of recovery usually require a *motivation* to heal, *patience, persistence, learning to tolerate emotional pain,* and learning about healthy *boundaries.* Then they can use the guidelines in the next chapter to make their own recovery plan.

Table 3. Potential Results of Unresolved Trauma*

Problems	Characteristics
Life	Trauma changes a normal life (e.g., may alter: beliefs, thoughts, feelings, decisions, choices, expectations, behaviors, relationships, vulnerabilities and life events); false self runs life
Relationship	Choosing friends who have been or feel victimized (instead of healthier ones); loss of friends; irritability/aggression/bullying; re-victimization; withdrawal; isolation; boundary problems
Thinking	Problems remembering and focusing; inhibited imagination, creativity, and choice-making ability; confusion; delayed information processing
Mental health	Chronic or complex PTSD; alcohol/other drug problems; behavior, mood, anxiety, somatoform, eating, sleep, impulse control, personality, dissociative, and/or psychotic disorders, including depression
Lessening/ numbing emotional pain	A style of confusion, self-distraction or distracting; alcohol or drug misuse or abuse; varying levels of dissociation; core recovery issues
Age regressions	Ordinary age regressions, sometimes with flashbacks and abreactions; dissociation, often leading to re-victimization
Repetitions (of the trauma)	Dangerous risk-taking; reenactments of aspects of the event, such as promiscuity or prostitution after molestation, or feeling choked and exhausted anytime adrenaline increased; provoking attacks
Self-punishment	Provoking attacks on self or others; low self-care; repeated dysfunctional choices in relationships, with problematic results;self-mutilation; isolation, suicidality
Repeated somatic complaints or illness	Aches and pains (e.g., abdominal and other body aches, including back pain, headaches); decreased immune response; functional and organic illness; disability; Doctors' office visits

* Expanded from Nader 2001; Felitti et al. 1998, Walker et al. 1999, McCaulley et al. 1997: see Whitfield 2003.

31

Q: What advice would you give a therapist who assists trauma survivors?

A: First, there is no therapist who does not see people who have suffered traumas. So we as therapists have to always have a high index of suspicion for the possibility that our patients or clients may have a trauma history.

I've seen such assisting work best when we listen carefully with our head *and* our heart. By listening with our head, I mean the knowledge that we have learned as therapists, including our ability to be objective. At the same time, we can listen with our heart, by which I mean listening to people's feelings, especially the painful feelings in their history, as they tell us their narrative or story.

I don't recommend treating with drugs too fast. The evidence that psychiatric drugs regularly help people is limited. In contrast to drugs like blood pressure medication, antibiotics and cardiac medications, most prescribed psychotropic drugs don't work very well for lessening chronic emotional pain. They have substantial side effects and they are expensive. Using them to treat trauma patients may focus on the drugs too much, distracting from the patients' main or real problems and their work to heal from them. That is not to say that some drugs at selected times are not appropriate.

Q: I have read that taking benzodiazepine drugs in the Xanax, Ativan, Valium family, may actually hinder treatment instead of help it. Is that true?

A: Yes, it is. These are actually *sedative* or *depressant* drugs (the drug companies appear to have made up the term "minor tranquilizers" as a sales gimmick), which have a high addiction potential, often numb people so much that they can't feel their other feelings, i.e., those feelings besides the anxiety or fear for which the drugs are being prescribed.

The code word for fear in our society has become

"anxiety." Nobody wants to call it what it is, i.e., fear, and not doing that dissociates both the clinician and the patient or client from the actual feeling. It sort of *mystifies* the whole experience, so that now the therapist or practitioner is the focus of being responsible for the healing process instead of the person who is suffering. The therapist is then expected to take fear away magically. Instead, people need to learn first what it is they are experiencing, give it an *accurate name,* and then learn *what* it may be *telling them,* and what to do with it or *how to process* it.

Q: Is there a common difficulty when working with trauma clients?

A: I think one of the biggest difficulties is having a feeling of being rushed, and focusing on the superficial. What most clinicians and many patients will understand is managed care's manipulation and intimidation. We also may not get to core issues because of our own inadequate training. Sometimes, some of the academics who teach our clinicians-in-training have not had much experience in clinical practice, or in their own personal healing.

Take, for example, one of the founders of family therapy, Murray Bowen, who many people worship to this day. One of the problems was, as fine a man as Dr. Bowen was, his main personal goal was to *individuate,* or separate himself from any of his own family-related emotional pain. Now this is a worthy goal. But I understand that he basically wanted to fix himself and his family without feeling the associated pain that naturally occurs when we do family-of-origin work. I would like to have that too, but it almost never works that way. As clinicians, we are too often in a hurry to make the patient's pain go away, when in fact the *pain* itself *may be a learning tool.*

So what we need is to help our patients learn skills to handle the pain. We need to assist them as they learn to tolerate the emotional pain, without self-medicating. Self-medicating can involve taking drugs or chemicals, like alcohol or prescribed pills, as well as food, work, smoking, gambling, sex and so on. There are other ways that people self-medicate, including by cutting and burning. Cutting and burning works at various levels to decrease pain, including by their stimulating a release of the body's natural painkillers called *endorphins* into the bloodstream.

But there is a difference between these kinds of potentially harmful ways of self-medicating and healthier ways of handling emotional pain, such as regular exercise, which we can call *self-soothing*. Other examples of self-soothing include *meditation, prayer, keeping a diary,* and going to *self-help meetings,* such as AA, NA (Narcotics Anonymous), Al-Anon, OA (Overeaters Anonymous), CoDA (Codependents Anonymous), and other self-help fellowships.

Q: What are some things you have learned in your practice that you would like to share with the readership?

A: One is the importance of knowing about the *stages of recovery,* which I describe throughout various sections of this book. I see four stages here, starting with Stage Zero. Stage Zero is active illness, and here recovery has not yet begun (Table 1 on page 2). In this stage, you see both symptoms and effects of whatever caused the illness. You may see the person suffering from addictions, disorders or illness. This could involve any mental or physical disease or problem. This stage can go on indefinitely—unless the person becomes somehow motivated to begin Stage One recovery.

Q: What is Stage One recovery?

A: Coming to treatment for any mental or physical disorder listed in any of the diagnostic codebooks is the beginning of Stage One. Stage One people come in with a presenting disorder that often is the effect of the trauma. This first stage is the standard kind of process that we most commonly consider as "treatment." If you are diabetic, you treat the diabetes by watching your diet, exercising, taking insulin, etc.

Another example of Stage One occurs with so-called mental illness: If somebody had "depression," they would often simply be prescribed an antidepressant drug, with little or no other investigation or intervention. Stage One is the conventional, superficial treatment of mental disorders, but it does not often work well.

Q: What is your opinion of brief therapy, given what you are saying about treatments that don't allow deeper exploration of the core issues?

A: That's fine, but the whole question is: Does it work? Where is the follow-up data on their studies? You need to do long follow-up prospective studies to prove that any therapy is going to work. Those quick-fix attempts don't often last if the person has had serious childhood trauma. Brief therapy may work for those with simple problems in living and who are otherwise stable.

Q: What is the typical motivation for beginning Stage One recovery?

A: Hurting too much. Emotional pain, physical pain or debilitating disease. But eventually, somewhere during or more often after Stage One recovery, people may realize that they are still hurting. They realize that whatever they have done before hasn't worked as well as they had hoped—that the Stage One approach alone didn't help them enough. So they might then become more open to exploring other alternatives. That is where they can begin this deeper healing—if they are lucky enough to find a helping professional who knows Stage Two work.

Q: How long does the Stage Two recovery process typically take?

A: For many people, it can take years for the recovery process, and for others it may take less. There is no judgment on the amount of time it takes a person to recover. In *A Gift to Myself*, I include numerous guidelines and experiential exercises to help facilitate Stage Two work, with a section at the end on how to assess when it may be time to stop therapy.

Q: What would you say to a person who can't do more therapy because of managed care, budget constraints, poverty and so on?

A: We do the best with what we have. People who are motivated to heal can be creative. That's one reason I wrote my books, i.e., for my patients, so they could save time and money by *learning* how to do the healing *themselves,* although with the help of safe others, including therapists. Often, people go from one therapist to another, like people do with attempted intimate relationships. They learn as much as they can with one teacher, and then go on to the next.

Q: In our clinic, we have had trauma clients say that "Other therapists didn't want to focus on what was underneath." I suppose this is evidence of these quick fixes you mention. With your long clinical experience, what other advice might you have?

A: People can be seductive. We would all probably like to learn how to do quick fixes. One of the dynamics here is that it makes us, as clinicians, feel more powerful and that we have thereby somehow transcended our own original pain.

Stage Two recovery is working with the effects of childhood and other trauma. Stage Two usually takes three to five years (give or take a few years) to work through it, and it takes a therapist who knows trauma and how to deal with it at this level. Therapists should ideally have done most of their own personal healing as well, so that they don't project too much of their own unfinished business onto their clients.

The second thing I would share is the need to name things accurately. Or re-framing them. If you want to read more about this, refer to the chapter "Naming Things Accurately" in my book *A Gift to Myself.* Instead of "depression," you can call it "grieving" from major losses and/or childhood trauma. And instead of saying "I deserved it," you can call it abuse or trauma.

Third, what we deal with in therapy is often actually grieving, or stuck, i.e., not moving, grief as it comes up, and not a mental disorder. A "mental disorder" involves Stage Zero and Stage One thinking, and stuck grief, i.e., needing to grieve but being blocked from doing it, would be Stage Two thinking and understanding. And of course, coming from that understanding is the need to help people identify what they are grieving from or about, and aid them in grieving in a healthy way.

Fourth, post-traumatic stress disorder (PTSD) is often a core problem in many who come to us for assistance. Making this accurate diagnosis helps the patient in a number of ways, including helping destigmatize the experience, symptoms and condition away from feeling unnecessary shame and guilt. It also helps with insurance coverage, since PTSD is in the diagnostic codebook.

The last advice is to realize the importance of spirituality in this whole process. Spirituality is a powerful tool. If the recovering person and the therapist do not understand spirituality, then one of the best places to go to learn about it is most any Twelve-Step group, no matter what the focus. Many people confuse spirituality with religion. While religions are kinds of "brand names," spirituality is the generic umbrella that embraces and transcends all religions. Psychological health is one of its goals. The healthier we are, the easier we can stay directly and authentically connected to ourselves and our Higher Power.

Q: What is Stage Three recovery?

A: Stage Three work is learning to realize spirituality. It is expanding the same question, "Who am I?" since that is a question central to Stage Two. In Stage Three, the person is continuing to work on "Who am I?" in a deeper way. And now we expand that question, "Who am I?" to the next interesting one: "What am I doing here?" and then "Where am I going?" Actually, Stage Three encompasses the whole process, from Stage Zero onward. Everything we do is spiritual, and by spiritual I am not talking about religion; I'm talking about *relationships* and *experiences* with self, others and the Universe or God/Goddess/All-That-Is.

Q: How do you see change occurring among the people you assist?

A: Many of my patients see that their health insurance coverage won't pay for ongoing recovery-related care, yet they are so committed to wanting to recover that they pay for it, financially as well as with their time and energy.

Q: What do you think makes you an effective psychotherapist?

A: My ability to see and function outside of the box of conventionality and narrow diagnostic and therapeutic thinking. This includes my ability to see through and not buy all of what some authority figures may recommend. As an example of the latter, I have had several patients for whom others have recommended electro-convulsive treatment (ECT) for their "depression." In all of these years, I have not seen a single patient who received ECT who benefited and was not

38

harmed by it in some way. I've also seen an increasing number of people who have been recommended to receive ECT who have researched its pluses and minuses and have declined. There are several Web sites now available that I've found helpful, and I just give them the Web sites to look up and read from, as well as a couple of Web sites that are pro-ECT, and they can decide for themselves. I give other examples of thinking and functioning outside of the box in *The Truth about Depression* and *The Truth about Mental Illness*.

I learned most of my clinical skills *after* I finished my conventional training. To do so, I had to be open to them. In this interview, I have described a sample of some of what I've learned. Here are some more bits of current, perhaps cutting-edge, information to consider.

In my over-twenty-five-years' experience, combined with my research of the peer-reviewed, published, data-based literature, I see a lot of evidence that mental illness is not actually caused by a genetically transmitted disorder of brain chemistry. Rather, what we call "mental illness" is actually commonly the *cumulative effect of trauma*. The one mental illness that has been studied the most is probably depression, and there are over 275 peer-reviewed, data-based studies that associate depression (and several other mental disorders) with trauma in a strong way, with statistically significant P values at less than .05 or .01 or .001. These are not trivial associations when you have a risk factor of two to twelve or more times the control group.

The association of mental illness (e.g., depression) with a child abuse history compared to controls, even when corrected for other confounding variables, can increase the risk factor for depression from two to twelve times (with a range of from two to twenty-five). And these reports involve a total of people studied in the many thousands. Some respected researchers, like Kenneth Kendler, a mostly genetics-oriented psychiatrist, now use the word *causal* in this regard, and not just "associated with." Other clinicians and researchers such as Colin Ross, Alvin Pam, Elliot Vallenstein and others also support my observations (see references).

The next most commonly reported disorder that has a strong association and high risk factor result with a history of childhood and later trauma is probably alcohol and other substance abuse problems, documented by well over 100 peer-reviewed published reports. Other mental disorders have also been studied and reported as being commonly associated with childhood trauma. Anxiety disorders, some personality disorders, and certainly aggressive and violent behaviors are strongly associated with a history of childhood trauma. Of the personality disorders, borderline personality disorder has the strongest association with childhood trauma, and some others also show significant associations.

Somatization disorder is one of the most commonly associated disorders with childhood trauma. The Adverse Childhood Experiences (ACE) study that I am working on at the Centers for Disease Control and Prevention has also shown these and numerous other medical problems to be associated with childhood trauma. In addition, if you take the ten leading causes of death in the United States, nearly every one has a high association with a history of childhood trauma as shown in *The Truth about Depression*.

This large-scale epidemiologic study—the ACE study— conducted jointly by the Centers for Disease Control (CDC, Atlanta) and Kaiser Permanente in San Diego, has found childhood abuse, including exposure to domestic violence, and related traumatic exposures to be the *norm* in this large sample of middle socioeconomic people (two-thirds of patients surveyed experienced at least one ACE, i.e., kind of childhood trauma). For example, the ACE study found that 16 percent of the men and more than one-fourth of women met the case definition for contact sexual abuse. In a recent nationally representative study of adults by researcher David Finkelhor and colleagues, 15 percent of men and more than 25 percent of women reported childhood sexual abuse. And

31 percent of the men in the ACE Study had been physically abused as boys, the same percentage found in a recent population-based study of Ontario, Canada, that used similar questions to define physical abuse.

If a child is exposed to one form of trauma, their probability of experiencing a second or third trauma is 80 percent and 50 percent, respectively, as epidemiologist Rob Anda, internist Vincent Felitti and their colleagues have pointed out. And, the effect of multiple childhood traumas, which are common, has repeatedly been shown to be cumulative for a variety of health and social problems. Therefore, it is important to use the uncovering of one childhood trauma as a possible clue to ask about others.

This information is but a sample of what is available on the trauma-illness link. I describe it in more detail in my companion books *The Truth about Depression* and *The Truth about Mental Illness*.

4

My Plan for
Stage Two Recovery

In the first section of this book, I described how to make such a plan for people with addictions, compulsions and other disorders. If you have any of these conditions that may be active now and may therefore distract you from your Stage Two recovery (healing from trauma effects), it may be useful to address them first. If you are uncertain, ask your therapist or counselor, if you are currently seeing one, for suggestions.

GETTING STARTED

To get somewhere, it's useful to know where you are going.

No matter what condition, concern or problem you are recovering from, you might already have some idea about what you want to happen—where you want to go—regarding that condition.

To accomplish what you want to happen in your recovery and in your life, it can be useful to make a Recovery Plan. (In a treatment facility or program, this may also be called a "treatment plan.")

Before beginning the recovery plan, let's review the process of recovery with emphasis on Stage Two recovery.

REVIEW OF RECOVERY

Realizing that the map is not the territory and that maps can be helpful, let's look at the map of recovery table. This reads from bottom to top.

Table 4. Recovery & Duration According to Stages

Recovery Stage	Condition	Focus of Recovery	Approximate Duration
3	**Human/ spiritual**	Spirituality	Ongoing
2	**Trauma effects**	Trauma-specific full recovery program	3 to 5 years
1	**Stage Zero disorder**	Basic-illness specific full recovery program	½ to 3 years
0	**Active illness**	Addiction, compulsion or disorder	Indefinite
		---------------------- Woundedness, trauma effects	

When to focus on Stages Two and Three recovery usually depends upon the person's prior healing and present condition.

STAGE ZERO

Stage Zero is manifested by the presence of active illness, such as an addiction, compulsion or another disorder. I described some of these disorders briefly in the first Recovery Plan guide. This active illness may be acute, or recurring or chronic. And without recovery, it may continue indefinitely. At Stage Zero, recovery hasn't yet started.

STAGE ONE

At Stage One, recovery begins. It involves participating in a full recovery program for whatever condition (Stage Zero) that you might have. This Stage One full recovery program assists you in healing any Stage Zero condition or disorder that you might have. I describe this process in chapter 14 of *A Gift to Myself* and chapter 10 of *Co-Dependence.*

STAGE TWO

Once you have a stable and solid Stage One recovery—one that has lasted for at least a year or longer—it may be time to consider looking into your Adult Child or trauma-effect issues (Stage Two recovery). By Adult Child, I mean anyone who grew up in an unhealthy, troubled or dysfunctional family. Many Adult Children of trauma may still be in a similar unhealthy environment, whether at home, in one or more relationships and/or at the workplace.

One major manifestation of these trauma effect issues is the now popular term *co-dependence.* While I and others have written elsewhere on co-dependence, my briefest definition is that it is any suffering and dysfunction associated with focusing on the needs and behavior of others. It is outer focusing to the detriment of self. As a primary effect of trauma, it usually underlies any and all of the addictions, compulsions and other disorders that I have briefly defined in My Recovery Plan for Stage One.

While the Adult Child syndrome and co-dependence do not cause most Stage Zero conditions, they do regularly aggravate them and often contribute to their relapse.

This Adult Child condition and co-dependence are caused by a wounding, which results in effects that covers the physical, mental, emotional and spiritual aspects of our being and life. Many trauma survivors also have post-traumatic stress disorder, which I address in *The Truth about Depression* and *The Truth about Mental Illness.*

As we learn about this wounding, rather than feeling as though we are bad, sick, crazy or stupid, we discover that we are none of these. Rather, we simply were and still are wounded. And our response to this wounding was not abnormal. It was actually an adaptive and normal reaction to the overly stressful situation of growing up in an unhealthy, troubled or dysfunctional family.

This normal reaction was both taught to us and learned by us. We learned it because it was all that was given to us and because it helped us to survive.

We know that what we learn, we can unlearn. We can get free of our unnecessary confusion and suffering around all of this. There is a way out.

You have probably already started on your way out in some fashion. Making this recovery plan will likely serve to facilitate and strengthen your overall recovery.

With the most complete full recovery program, Stage Two recovery usually takes from three to five years to complete. For many people, it may take longer. There is absolutely no rush or need to hurry your recovery. Take as long as you need.

STAGE THREE

Stage Three recovery is spirituality. You may have already begun to incorporate it into your life. I describe this in my workshops and tapes on spirituality, and briefly in *Healing the Child Within, A Gift to Myself* and *Co-Dependence.*

I will also show how to use this spiritual part of recovery in my recovery plan for Stage Three.

If I identify with being an Adult Child of trauma and wish to explore the recovery process, I can begin by considering how I might create my own personal recovery plan.

CREATING MY RECOVERY PLAN

In creating my personal recovery plan, I can ask myself three questions:

1. What are my *problems, issues* or *concerns?* What do I *want to change* about my life now?

2. Given these problems, what do I *want to happen?*

3. How can *I accomplish* what I want to happen?

Naming My Problems and Issues

What are my problems, issues or concerns? What do I want to change about my life now?

In answering this first question, it is useful to begin to name what my problems, issues or concerns might be in my life right now.

I may be hurting in some way, feeling frustrated about or unfulfilled in my relationships or feeling sad or empty. While the list of possible problems is long, we can perhaps derive some assistance in naming our problems by looking at which issues tend to be most common among trauma survivors.

An *issue* is any conflict, concern or potential problem, whether conscious or unconscious, that is incomplete for us—or that needs action or change. A core issue is one that comes up repeatedly for many of us. There are at least fourteen core issues. These include:

CORE ISSUES

- Control
- Trust
- Being real
- Feelings
- Dependence
- Fear of abandonment
- All-or-none thinking and behaving
- High tolerance for inappropriate behavior
- Low self-esteem
- Over-responsibility for others
- Neglecting my own needs
- Grieving my ungrieved losses
- Difficulty resolving conflict
- Difficulty giving love and receiving love

These core issues tend to emerge especially from several areas of our recovery and life:

- Relationships—of any kind—with others, self and our Higher Power
- Doing experiential recovery work—throughout our healing
- Feedback given by our therapy group members, therapists, sponsors, friends and others
- Insight from reading, listening, reflecting upon or working through conflict

Core issues can assist us in describing and framing some of the origins and dynamics of such concepts as our:

- Problems in living
- Day-to-day conflicts
- "Character defects"
- Our struggle with our ego or false self (co-dependent self)

Are there any of these core issues or concerns with which you can identify? Underline or make a check mark next to any of these. If you choose, write any reactions or comments that you may have about any of these in the space below.

_____

_____

_____

_____

_____

_____

Of these, are there any that you would particularly like to work on? Draw a circle around any of these.

Perhaps you have an issue, problem or concern that is not on this above list. Or something else about your life now that you want to change. Here is some space to name or describe anything that might come up for you.

_____

_____

_____

_____

_____

_____

Of these additions above, are there any that you would particularly like to work on now? Draw a circle around any of these.

As any issues, problems or concerns may come up for you in the future, or as any clarification on any of the above comes up, add them. Below there is some space for doing this.

_____

_____

_____

_____

_____

_____

_____

_____

_____

_____

_____

_____

Once we have identified and named our issues, we have started our recovery plan. All we have to do now is to write these onto the left side of our blank recovery plan on page 51. (Space these out equally or write them in pencil so you can move them around on the page later.)

At this point, be aware of all-or-none thinking or behaving (i.e., trying to do all and heal all at once, or giving up on recovery altogether in frustration because you may feel overwhelmed or hopeless). If you have a long list of issues upon which you want to work, it is most useful at this point to prioritize the list by numbering them as "1" for your most important, "2" for your second most important and so on. Keep your complete list for later and start out with your first three. Keeping it simple like this will allow you to focus on making your recovery plan and on your overall recovery.

READER/CUSTOMER CARE SURVEY

We care about your opinions. Please take a moment to fill out this Reader Survey card and mail it back to us.
As a special **"thank you"** we'll send you exciting news about interesting books and a valuable **Gift Certificate.**

Please PRINT using ALL CAPS

First Name [   ] MI. [ ] Last Name [   ]

Address [   ]

City [   ] ST [ ] Zip [   ]

Phone # ([   ]) [   ] — [   ]   Fax # ([   ]) [   ] — [   ]

Email [   ]

(1) Gender:
_____ Female   _____ Male

(2) Age:
1) _____ 12 or under
2) _____ 13-19
3) _____ 20-39
4) _____ 40-59
5) _____ 60+

(3) Marital Status
_____ Married
_____ Single
_____ Divorced/Widowed

(4) Did you receive this book as a gift?
_____ Yes   _____ No

(5) How many Health Communications books have you bought or read?
_____ 1   _____ 2-4   _____ 5+

(6) How did you find out about this book?
Please fill in ONE.
1) _____ Recommendation
2) _____ Store Display
3) _____ Bestseller List
4) _____ Online
5) _____ Advertisement
6) _____ Catalog/Mailing
7) _____ Interview/Review (TV, Radio, Print)

(7) Where do you usually buy books?
Please fill in your top TWO choices.
1) _____ Bookstore
2) _____ Religious Bookstore
3) _____ Online
4) _____ Book Club/Mail Order
5) _____ Price Club (Costco, Sam's Club, etc.)
6) _____ Retail Store (Target, Wal-Mart, etc.)

(9) What subjects do you enjoy reading about most? Rank only *FIVE.* Use 1 for your favorite, 2 for *second favorite, etc.*

	1	2	3	4	5
1) Parenting/Family	○	○	○	○	○
2) Relationships	○	○	○	○	○
3) Recovery/Addictions	○	○	○	○	○
4) Health/Nutrition	○	○	○	○	○
5) Christianity	○	○	○	○	○
6) Spirituality/Inspiration	○	○	○	○	○
7) Business Self-Help	○	○	○	○	○
8) Teen Issues	○	○	○	○	○
9) Sports	○	○	○	○	○

(14) What attracts you most to a book?
(Please rank 1-4 in order of preference.)

	1	2	3	4
1) Title	○	○	○	○
2) Cover Design	○	○	○	○
3) Author	○	○	○	○
4) Content	○	○	○	○

BB1

TAPE IN MIDDLE; DO NOT STAPLE

NO POSTAGE
NECESSARY
IF MAILED
IN THE
UNITED STATES

BUSINESS REPLY MAIL

FIRST-CLASS MAIL PERMIT NO 45 DEERFIELD BEACH, FL

POSTAGE WILL BE PAID BY ADDRESSEE

HEALTH COMMUNICATIONS, INC.
3201 SW 15TH STREET
DEERFIELD BEACH FL 33442-9875

FOLD HERE

Comments:

MY RECOVERY PLAN

Name (optional) _____ Date _____

Problem or Condition	What I Want to Happen (Goals)	How I Plan to Reach These Goals

WHAT DO I WANT TO HAPPEN?

Given these problems, issues or concerns, what do I want to happen?

If I feel chronically unhappy, what I may want to happen is to experience some happiness and serenity. If I have low self-esteem and feel a lot of shame, I may want to experience less shame and a higher self-esteem. Since these are examples of some goals that I may want to reach, I can call "What I want to happen" a recovery goal.

In *Healing the Child Within*, I briefly described the four main goals of healing and of Adult Child, co-dependence and trauma recovery. They are as follows:

1. Discover and practice being our Real Self or Child Within.
2. Identify our needs. These needs are ongoing throughout our lives and include our physical, mental, emotional and spiritual needs. We practice getting these needs met alone, with safe and supportive people, and if we choose, with our Higher Power.
3. Identify, re-experience and grieve the pain of our ungrieved losses or traumas in the presence of safe and supportive people.
4. Identify and work through our core issues, which I describe here, and also in *Healing the Child Within* and *A Gift to Myself*.

These actions are closely related, although they are not listed in any particular order. Working on them, and thereby healing our Child Within, generally occurs in a circular fashion, with work and discovery in one area being a link to another area.

Working in these four areas—with a progressively increasing awareness and experience—constitutes the healing process.

The preceding four examples of overall recovery goals might correspond with the following problems or issues numerically: (1) I don't know who I really am. (2) Difficulty knowing and getting my needs met. (3) Difficulty knowing and handling my feelings. (4) I often feel overwhelmed with problems.

If you are ready, next to each problem or issue that you have written in the left column on page 51, write what you want to happen. There is no need to rush in this process. Take all the time you need. If you would like some assistance, ask your therapist or counselor. (If you don't have one, you might want to consider having a consultation with one. Ask your trusted friends and/or look at the bottom of page 117 and pages 130–132 in *A Gift to Myself* about how to find a therapist or counselor.)

SOME OVERALL RECOVERY GOALS— WHAT I WANT TO HAPPEN

In *A Gift to Myself* (page 118), I have written eleven long-term recovery goals and have added six principles for using them (items 12–17 as follows). I list these here not to encourage you to use these exact goals, but as more material to stimulate your thinking, planning and recovery.

LONG-TERM RECOVERY GOALS FOR
ADULT CHILDREN OF TRAUMA

Self-Awareness
1. Discover, develop and accept my personal and individual identity as separate from my spouse or partner, parental or other authority figure, children and institutions.
2. Identify my ongoing needs (physical, mental, emotional and spiritual).

Self-Acceptance
3. Practice getting these needs met on my own and with safe people in healthy relationships.
4. Identify, trust and process my internal cues (feelings, sensations and experience from my inner life). If not comfortable, check my responses with someone I trust.
5. Assess my feelings, upsets, conflicts and similar situations and handle them in a healthy way (alone, with safe others and, if I choose, with my Higher Power).
6. Learn to accept myself as an individual and unique child of God, with strengths and weaknesses.
7. Learn to like myself and eventually to love myself, as my Higher Power loves me.

Self-Responsibility
8. Identify, re-experience and grieve the pain of ungrieved losses, hurts or mistreatment, alone and with safe others.
9. Identify and work through my major core recovery issues.
10. Grieve the loss of my childhood while in group.
11. Develop and use an ongoing support system (at least three supports).

Self-Reflection

12. There is no hurry for me to accomplish these goals right away. I can take my time.
13. I don't have to reach every goal perfectly.
14. I do not have to work on these goals in exactly this order.
15. From these above goals, I will—in my own time—make more specific and more personal goals for myself during my recovery.
16. I can accomplish these goals through techniques such as risking and telling my story to safe people, through prayer and meditation, keeping a journal and other experiential techniques.
17. Using the above, I am caring for and healing my True Self.

You can use these goals and reflections to stimulate your thinking about your specific needs in your recovery.

If you have not written any goals on pages 51 or 64 that are personal and meaningful to you or if you want to add some more goals, you can practice writing these on blank paper. When you have had some time to reflect upon and digest these, you can prioritize them and then write them into the appropriate space on page 63. Remember that to make your recovery more healing, each goal or set of goals ("What I want to happen") should correspond to the problem or condition that you have written to its left on page 64.

REACHING THESE GOALS

How can I accomplish what I want to happen?

Having written your problems and concerns, plus your recovery goals, you can begin to consider how you can specifically accomplish reaching these goals. These methods of accomplishment are also called objectives. They may include many different possibilities of action including:

POSSIBLE RECOVERY AIDS

- Attending and participating in a therapy group
- Attending and participating in a self-help group (such as Adult Children or Co-dependents Anonymous and/or Al-Anon)
- Individual counseling or psychotherapy
- Reading selected recovery-related literature, also called *bibliotherapy*
- Participating in an intensive weekend or residential experience
- Reading and working through an Adult Child of trauma–oriented workbook such as *A Gift to Myself*
- Keeping and writing in a diary or journal regularly
- Sharing important aspects of my inner life, especially including feelings with a trusted and safe other
- Using any one or more experiential recovery techniques (described on pages 139–166 of *A Gift to Myself*)
- Any creative recovery method that I can create

A characteristic of an ideal recovery aid or objective is that it is measurable. That is, you can account for it in some way, such as by the number of times, frequency or regularity that you attended, shared, read, completed or otherwise accomplished what you planned to accomplish. Examples: "Attend group therapy weekly," "Attend self-help group twice a week," or "Share at least one feeling each day with a safe person."

Whenever you have some time, begin to consider: How can I specifically accomplish what I want to happen?

For each goal that you have written on page 64 or elsewhere, write how you plan to accomplish that goal.

Remember to keep it simple. A characteristic of some trauma survivors is that they tend to bite off more than they can chew—to commit to more than they really want or agree to. At the same time, it is useful to include as many methods or objectives that would be the most helpful in reaching a particular goal. If you have any questions, ask your therapist or counselor.

To assist you further in writing your recovery plan, here is an example.

SAMPLE TREATMENT OR RECOVERY PLAN

Problem or Condition	What I Want to Happen (Goals)	How I Plan to Reach These Goals
Chronic unhappiness	Experience some peace, happiness or serenity.	1. Begin to heal my Child Within.
Low self-esteem	Raise my self-esteem.	2. Make a long-term commitment to an Adult Child–specific therapy group.
		3. Attend that group weekly and work on a personal problem or issue at least monthly.
		4. Whenever it comes up, share about my low self-esteem and shame.

Problem or Condition	What I Want to Happen (Goals)	How I Plan to Reach These Goals
Difficulty with intimate relationships	Improve my participation in my intimate relationships. Have one successful intimate relationship.	1. Practice 1 to 4 above. 2. Work on my relationship problems in group therapy. 3. Keep a diary or journal about my experiences in relationships. 4. Seek individual therapy with a therapist knowledgeable in Adult Child recovery.

PROGRESSING IN RECOVERY

It usually takes a while to develop a stable recovery from trauma effects (page 31). For example, I have seen many recovering people take from one to two years just to begin getting to know what their feelings are and how they really feel. And there is absolutely nothing wrong with this.

Overall, it takes about three to five years—or longer—in a full recovery program to reach a successful recovery. So give yourself plenty of time.

Recovery is not an intellectual or rational process. Nor is it easy. It is mostly an experiential process, consisting of excitement, discouragement, pain and joy, and with an overall pattern of personal growth. Recovery takes great courage. Even though it cannot be explained adequately with words alone,

I have begun to describe the process of recovery in *Healing the Child Within, A Gift to Myself* and *Memory and Abuse*. By making and maintaining a recovery plan, we can make our recovery progress with greater awareness and more success.

REVISING AND UPDATING MY RECOVERY PLAN

It is useful to place a copy of your recovery plan in a prominent place, yet safe from prying eyes, where you can see it every day. Read it over carefully every week.

Every few months, review it based on how your recovery is progressing and make any changes you might consider useful. You can ask your therapist, counselor or therapy group for suggestions here. It would be helpful to read your recovery plan to your therapy group, if you are in one, and ask for their feedback and their assistance in reaching your goals.

Working on and through a particular problem, concern or issue is usually a step-by-step process that proceeds over several weeks, months or years. As we work through a specific core recovery issue, we can do so in an evolutionary sequence, depending on where we might be in our healing around that particular core issue. For example:

1. Early in such evolution, we may be most interested in such healing actions as questioning, risking, realizing, recognizing, identifying and defining.
2. In the middle stage of our healing around a core issue, we may use learning, practicing, clarifying, experiencing and working at a deeper level.
3. During an advanced stage, we may begin to consolidate our progressively increasing awareness around the core issue, while using that awareness by working through upsets and conflicts without being a martyr or victim,

but rather as a Hero/Heroine (see *A Gift to Myself,* pages 188, 190 and 212).

4. When we are recovered, we can continue using all of the above with still more awareness, success and enjoyment.

I expand our working through these core recovery issues into these four stages on pages 62 and 63.

COMPLETION OF AN ACTIVE
FULL RECOVERY PROGRAM

While experiencing, working, learning and growing continue throughout our lives, there may come a time when we have completed most of our Stage Two recovery work. This will be when we can consider slowing or stopping the frequency and intensity of our active full recovery program. How to assess and determine that point is not easy. I have written some guidelines for doing so in chapter 29 (pages 245–250) of *A Gift to Myself.*

STAGE THREE RECOVERY

While Stage Three recovery, or spirituality, can be started at any time during recovery, it can now be used more constructively. This is because the only part of us that can experientially connect to God is our True Self—our Child Within.

I describe using spirituality in recovery in the last chapter of *Healing The Child Within,* chapter 27 of *A Gift to Myself,* and in chapter 12 of this book.

I wish you all the best on your journey of recovery.

MY RECOVERY PLAN

Name (optional) _____ Date _____

Problem or Condition	What I Want to Happen (Goals)	How I Plan to Reach These Goals

Table 5. Some Steps in Transforming and Integrating Core Recovery Issues in Stage Two Recovery

Issues	Early	Middle	Advanced	Recovered
1. Grieving	Identifying our losses	Learning to grieve	Grieving	Grieving current losses
2. Being real	Identifying our Real Self	Risking being real	Practicing being real	Being real
3. Neglecting our own needs	Realizing we have needs	Identifying our needs	Beginning to get our needs met	Getting our needs met
4. Being over-responsible for others, etc	Identifying boundaries	Clarifying boundaries	Learning to set limits	Being responsible for self, with clear boundaries
5. Low self-esteem	Identifying	Sharing	Affirming	Improved self-esteem
6. Control	Identifying	Beginning to let go	Taking responsibility	Taking responsibility while letting go
7. All-or-none	Recovering and identifying	Learning both/and choices	Getting free	Freedom from all-or-none choices

(continued on next page)

Table 5. Some Steps in Transforming and Integrating Core Recovery Issues in Stage Two Recovery

Issues	Early	Middle	Advanced	Recovered
8. Trust	Realizing trusting can be helpful	Trusting selectively	Learning to trust safe people	Trusting appropriately
9. Feeling	Recognizing and identifying	Experiencing	Using	Observing and using feelings
10. High tolerance for in appropriate behavior	Questioning what is appropriate and what is not	Learning what is appropriate and what is not	Learning to set limits	Knowing what is appropriate, or if not, asking a safe person
11. Fear of abandonment	Realizing we were abandoned or neglected	Talking about it	Grieving our abandonment	Freedom from fear of abandonment
12. Difficulty handling and resolving conflict	Recognizing and risking	Practicing expressing feelings	Resolving conflicts	Working through current conflicts
13/ 14. Difficulty giving and receiving love	Defining love	Practicing love	Forgiving and refining	Loving self, others and Higher Power
15. Dependence	Identifying our dependence needs	Learning about healthy dependence and healthy independence	Practicing healthy dependence and independence	Being healthily dependent and independent

Source: *A Gift to Myself*

MY RECOVERY PLAN

Name (optional) _____ Date _____

Problem or Condition	What I Want to Happen (Goals)	How I Plan to Reach These Goals

5

An Introduction to Recovery and Spirituality

AN INTERVIEW WITH CHARLES WHITFIELD, M.D.,
BY BARBARA WHITFIELD, R.T., C.M.T.

In the next eight chapters, Barbara Whitfield interviews Charles Whitfield about how using spirituality can help recovery. They also address the Twelve Steps in some introductory principles, and finally mention the modern holy book, *A Course in Miracles*.

DEFINING ADDICTION

Barbara Whitfield: You have reframed addiction and mental illness as part of the hero's journey, which the mythologist and author Joseph Campbell and others have talked about.

When people enter Stage Two recovery, it may no longer be useful for them to think of themselves as having a disease or a DSM label (from the *Diagnostic and Statistical Manual* of the American Psychiatric Association). When we are working on healing from our wounds, as you say, it is freeing to reframe them as part of our journey to wholeness.

In this context, how do you define addiction? What does it mean to be addicted?

Charles Whitfield: To be addicted means to cling to something, to be attached to something to one's detriment. The simplest definition I've heard was "recurring trouble," recurring trouble associated with being in relationship with anything, any person, place, thing, behavior or experience the person might be involved in. So, addiction is really a relationship problem. It's a problem about our various relationships with people, places and things.

THE ROLE OF TRAUMA

Q: Co-dependence was a term that came to us from the 1980s. Some have criticized it for being too nonspecific. How would you define it?

A: Co-dependence focuses that same definition as for addiction, but now more on our relationships with *people*. Using it can be helpful at times, mostly to abbreviate, clarify and help us describe *relationship addictions*. Underlying nearly all addictions is co-dependence and a history of childhood trauma. Co-dependence and other trauma effects are underpinnings or an underbase of all addiction, it seems to me. I've never met a person who was addicted to alcohol or other drugs who grew up in a healthy family and who was not also and underneath co-dependent. It's another word for the "neurosis of our time."

Co-dependence means focusing on others to one's detriment. That can be expanded to the entire definition of addiction I just mentioned, which is focusing outside of oneself anywhere to one's detriment; onto people, places, things, behaviors and experiences. Co-dependence has multiple manifestations and dynamics. Co-dependence is the human condition. It's what over the centuries and millennia we've been talking about, this thing called "The Human Condition." Co-dependence is the closest thing to giving us an answer to or a clear explanation of that concern that I've been able to find. Co-dependence usually comes from being abused or neglected as a child, and is later aggravated by experiencing trauma as an adult.

Q: Does that mean everyone is co-dependent in some sense?

A: Most people grew up in a troubled, unhealthy or dys-functional family. "Most" meaning probably 70 to 90 percent of the population. That's the way a person gets co-dependent. They grow up in this family and world where they are trau-matized, and to survive they learn to be co-dependent. To help them survive, they learn all these various ways of losing awareness of their real self. Dissociating from the true self, to survive the traumas, we come to rely on letting our false self run our life, and we become unhealthily dependent on others.

Q: Then would co-dependence make a person vulnerable to becoming addicted?

A: Co-dependence is a major manifestation of being trau-matized as a child and then growing up to become what we have called an Adult Child of a dysfunctional family. That co-dependence is one way to begin to describe some of the *effects* of the *trauma*. This Adult Child wounding is what underlies most addictions.

In my research and my clinical experience, I found strong to overwhelming evidence that the childhood abuse and neglect has a significant association with common mental ill-ness and some physical illness.*

People who develop an addiction can get into a recovery program through a Stage One full recovery program. Doing that usually takes one to three years for them to get stabilized. And for an addiction, working the Twelve Steps is a useful

---

*I summarize and discuss this link in my two books, *The Truth about Depression* and *The Truth about Mental Illness.* There I present more than 300 clinical and scientific databased, peer-reviewed published reports that document the strong and at times causal link between childhood trauma and subsequent illness, including addictions.

way to get that started. Then, somewhere along the line, they may decide to go into a deeper recovery, which I call Stage Two recovery. There, over time, they can work on the other effects of their trauma, i.e., their co-dependence, their Adult Child issues, which are simply the effects of the repeated trauma. More people are doing that nowadays.

Stage Three recovery begins somewhere toward the end of that Stage Two healing. That is the stage of spirituality—becoming more and more spiritually aware and spiritually connected with self, others and Higher Power, or God/Goddess/All-That-Is.

SPIRITUALITY

Q: As a physician, you originally focused on addiction recovery and trauma effects. But you have expanded beyond the traditional medical model. As a respiratory therapist, I observed physicians focusing only on Stages Zero and One. They seemed to believe that healing ended there. But soon our patients returned with a relapse or something else wrong that was related. And I'm not just referring to addiction here. Our patients were returning with one physical ailment after another. From your experience as a physician, can you tell us how that happens?

A: I continued to look in my practice of medicine for answers to help people in their recoveries from anything. I started out in general medicine and internal medicine–conventional medicine. I looked for answers for how to help people in their recoveries—beyond what I had originally learned in my medical school and residency and fellowship training.

So I was constantly exploring what might help people. And then in 1973 I saw a particular alcoholic man who came in with his family. I started to learn the importance of the family. And I began learning the importance of using the Twelve Steps in recovery. I saw that those Twelve Steps did not address just the physical or the mental. But they addressed more—the physical, mental, *emotional* and *spiritual*. I've noticed now, over the last twenty-five years, that the recovery movement has developed from what I like to call "the old paradigm," which includes just the physical and mental. It's a movement into what could be called "the new paradigm," which is not just physical and mental, but embraces also the emotional and spiritual. It includes it all—physical, mental, emotional and spiritual.

THE SEARCH FOR SELF AND GOD

Q: So Stage Two recovery work picks up where conventional medicine stops. But why include the emotional and spiritual? Western medicine has always relegated the spiritual to the church and its clergy. Why bother with the spiritual?

A: We're all searching to find meaning and fulfillment in our lives. And that search may involve addiction. I think addiction is part of the search. People have called addiction and some other illnesses "an escape." My sense is that it is not limited to trying to avoid pain. I believe that it is more. Addiction, co-addictions, co-dependence and some other mental illnesses are also about a search, and the search is for self and God. And self's connection to God—and God's connection to self. What happens, though, is that self, when it goes into hiding because it grew up in a hostile family of origin and a hostile world, that True Self, which I also call "the Child Within," goes into hiding, which brings about the feeling of emptiness. And then it becomes harder to connect to God. We can't connect to our Higher Power very effectively, successfully. That's another major reason for our feeling of emptiness. Feeling so empty, we search for anything that will

69

fill our needs. That goes right back to the people, places, things, behaviors and experiences that we've all looked for and gotten into relationship with, even addicted relationships. And that frustrates us, because those relationships don't fulfill us, at least not for very long. They may work for a few seconds, minutes, hours, days, weeks—a short time, but not long enough.

The problem is that these people, places and things will not fill our emptiness for very long—until we get so frustrated that we start looking elsewhere. And finally, we look within, and we look to the spiritual. And there we begin to get a sense of the spiritual—if we persist. But it may take a long time and we often get frustrated in that search. Eventually, we might start to feel some fulfillment. We may begin to feel some peace.

As we continue in our recoveries using this new paradigm approach (which is actually not all that new), physical, mental, emotional and spiritual, using the Twelve Steps, using group therapy, individual counseling, whatever it takes—or better—a combination, then we start to feel progressively more fulfilled. Our emptiness starts to go away, because the original cause of the emptiness wasn't an absence of alcohol—or a drug—or food—or work—or you name it! *The cause of the emptiness was our temporary loss of our True Self and its experiential connection to God.* And when we reclaim, when we recognize, when we remember our True Self and become it again, and start living as it, our emptiness begins to go away. Our emptiness gets even less, because we can now experientially connect to God more easily.

The only part of us that can connect to God or our Higher Power is our True Self. Our false self, our co-dependent self can't do that. That false self is what AA talks about as "King Baby," "the grandiose self," "the big I." It is our ego. When we are in our ego we cannot connect to God.

Q: Then, is the only part of us that can connect to God

experientially (not just in our head, as our ego may pretend) our True Self, our Child Within?

A: Yes. One of our teachers said that to get into the kingdom of heaven we have to become like a little child. And so, once we have begun to realize our True Self, we then experientially connect to the God of our understanding, and then the emptiness begins to go away. It goes away progressively more and more, and we feel empty less and less.

Q: So, are addictions and other problems symptomatic of this painful search?

A: Is the addiction part of the whole process of the search for self and God? My answer is yes, it is. The addiction and the co-dependence are part of the Divine Mystery, the Divine Plan, it seems. To choose self and God authentically, we have to have something to choose *instead* of them. And so first we try all of these other people, places and things—and they don't work. They frustrate us. And so the addictions and other problems are ways that frustrate us, but paradoxically they also are gifts that allow us to make an authentic choice for self and God. As Gerald May said, *If we didn't have those, our choice would not be authentic.*

Q: So should we all become addicted?

A: Well, I don't think so, but given our usual circumstances, people are going to get attached and cling to some things no matter what. Unless they are a realized spiritual master when they are born, and most people aren't. So, I think that's part of the human journey, the human adventure—to get attached to things that end up frustrating us. They don't fulfill us. Then we have to go on this search—that turns out to be for self and God.

Q: So a comforting reframe here would be to see addiction as a gift, a search for our True Self or what you call the Child Within. And then we find that growth in recovery can be part of it, too.

A: Yes. Addiction, which seemed to be a curse, turns out to be a gift in disguise in recovery. But before a more full recovery it still often feels like a curse.

In the next section, let's look at some of the healing actions of the Twelve Steps of Alcoholics Anonymous and the some 100 other self-help fellowships that have adopted them.

6

The Twelve Steps

These questions and answers can be kind of a background to using the Twelve Steps in healing. Let's look at those steps here.

THE FIRST STEP

Barbara Whitfield: Step One says that "We admitted that we were powerless over alcohol (or it could be some other substance or behavior), that our lives had become unmanageable." Why do the Twelve Steps start with such a seemingly pessimistic kind of admission?

Charles Whitfield: I don't see that First Step as pessimistic or negative. I see it as painful, as humbling, becoming vulnerable, becoming real and honest—but not negative. Some people call feelings "negative feelings" and "positive feelings." I don't find that view very useful. I like to call them *painful* and *joyful* feelings. And so, this is a painful step to take, this First Step—admitting powerlessness and unmanageability. I think there are several key words in this step. The first one is *We*. It implies that we can't do it alone. And of course, the paradox there is that: (1) we can't do it alone. We need safe others in recovery, *and* (2) the only way we can do it ultimately is with our own internal resources, i.e., alone. Now those internal resources are part of our spiritual strength in our recovery, including our potential experiential connection to God.

Q: When I said "pessimistic" I was thinking in terms of the opposite of the power of optimistic or positive thinking.

A: Well, that may be that idea of doing it on our own. It may be part of the trap of the human condition. And that taps right into the core recovery issue of *control*—needing to be in control. The First Step addresses it directly. It says, "I'm not in control. I am not in charge. I am indeed powerless over whatever I'm clinging to—whatever I'm attached to in an unhealthy way."

Q: What's the importance here of the issue of control, which is so frequently talked about by recovering people?

A: To me, the basis for control is our attachment to our false self, to our ego, or negative ego. That's "King Baby," the grandiose self, the co-dependent self. One of its characteristics is that it thinks that, and it behaves as though it must be in control. It has to be in control because that's the only way it can think it amounts to anything.

Q: Then, is an excessive need for control a kind of defense mechanism, a sign of insecurity?

A: Needing to be in control is a way to defend against emotional pain. Controlling our feelings, our emotions, what's coming up for us from our inner life—needing to control it and them. All of that is on the one hand useful, because most of these so-called "ego defenses" have some usefulness. But they are double-edged swords, too, because they have some detrimental or destructive qualities. And, of course, that is controlling something to the extent that it ends up harming *us*—the very person who's trying to do the controlling. That's what nearly every addict and co-dependent eventually does. That's why control is a core recovery issue.

Q: We can see their relief and improvement when recovering people work over time in a self-help fellowship and group therapy. So why do so many people deny their addiction?

Why do people deny their other disorders, including some mental disorders, and co-dependence?

A: On first examining it, denial might look like the person is lying or trying to cover up or won't admit having difficulty with their person, place or thing of choice. But it's more complex. It's not all about willpower. Willpower is related to control here. Willpower is a guise of false self. It is the assumed "power" of the false self. And it doesn't work well for recovery from addictions. We have to discover that fact from our repeated frustrations. Denial has much more in its dynamics than just lying, covering up or being dishonest. It has to do much more with what Leclair Bissell, M.D., and others have called: 1) toxic properties of the substance, 2) not wanting to be found out, 3) not wanting to feel our shame, hurt or fear, and also just 4) ignorance of the problem.

Unfortunately, we're not born into a family that explains all of this to us. Our parents and teachers often explain the opposite. So we have to go out into the world and find out for ourselves what addictions and other life problems are all about. And we end up having some not-so-good teachers along the way, until finally we get into recovery where we can learn at a deeper level. And as we learn, we address that ignorance. We then find out progressively more truth, until now we say, "Oh yeah! Is that what happened? It's a disease. It was not my fault. I didn't cause it." And if you don't want to call it a disease, call it a disorder or a problem or whatever you want. It's a process that has overtaken me. Then I can begin to understand that toxic process more and more clearly, and eventually I can learn to let go of my need to keep it at bay or deny it.

Q: So an addict is not a bad person?

A: Absolutely not. Not at all. The addicted, disordered or distressed person is not bad, sick, crazy or stupid. What I

prefer to call it is that they are just "wounded." These symptoms, signs and behaviors are just some of the painful effects
of the trauma that wounded them that was not expressed and
validated when it happened. The pain is also commonly *not
allowed* by their abusers and enablers to be expressed and the
abusers frequently invalidate that the abuse even happened.
So they grow up believing that they, the trauma victims, are
the problem, when actually they are simply suffering the
effects of trauma by their abusers and enablers. They're
wounded and they're searching—like most of us appear to be
doing in one way or another.

THE SECOND STEP

Q: Step Two says that we "Came to believe that a power
greater than ourselves could restore us to sanity." What does
"the power greater than ourselves" mean here? And what
does sanity mean?

A: Sanity to me is being whole, being holy, having wholeness, being complete—and that includes physical, mental,
emotional and spiritual parts of our wholeness. And so sanity means having a healthy and growing sense of self in those
four realms. And so, in *restore us to sanity* then—Higher
Power assists us in that restoration as we get closer to self-
actualization, as Maslow called it, or sanity, as the step says.
Of course, it's all God.

Now, *the power greater than ourselves* could be anything. It
doesn't have to be limited to one thing, like some religious
groups' God that says you have to believe this way or that.
It's the God *of our understanding* that's important here. It's the
Higher Power of our understanding—God/Goddess/All-
That-Is, Allah, Yahweh, The Great Spirit—whatever works,
whatever will help us realize our wholeness.

Q: Do recovering people have a kind of opportunity to relate to a Higher Power directly, which many people call God, that meets their needs?

A: Yes. The Second Step gives us the opportunity and encouragement to find something outside of our false self, outside of our co-dependent self that might have some answers. I'm suggesting that our two parts—two major forces that have the answer—are our True Self and its Higher Power. It's our *connection* with our Higher Power. That working together of True Self, who we really are, with the God of its understanding—is the powerful co-creation process.

THE THIRD STEP

Q: So we are forming a real relationship with our real self, and at the same time with God—in a way that feels authentic in our own inner life. Which brings us to Step Three. It says we "Made a decision to turn our will and our lives over to the care of God as we understood God." How does that step flow from the first two? Where does it fit into the overall process?

A: The problem that I see a lot of people get into with the Third Step is that they may gloss over that word *care*—the *care* of God. And so it's not saying that we have to turn our will or our life *completely* over to God—but only to the *care* of God. You see, we're still in charge here, in the sense that we can still choose at any time we want. We still have free will. We can choose God or anything other than God. In part, that's what *A Course in Miracles* says. The "Course" has helped many spiritual seekers, myself included, to know self, others and God better. I'll say more about it later.

As we co-create, we are more powerful when we choose God. But first, we've got to do our own stuff, our own work. We've got to handle our own difficulties as they come up, our own problems and conflicts. We become *aware* of our conflicts, problems and our concerns. We *feel* them. We *work* them. We *share* our work with safe people to heal. And that's where others come in, safe others. We might want to write or journal about it. Sleep on it. We might meditate on it—pray about it. Whatever may work for us to help us self-discover and heal.

Then, as we work through the pain and the upset of that particular problem or conflict that happened now in our life, we can come to a point where we can realize, "That's about all I can do. I've done as much as I can do now. I've really worked on this thing. I've worked on it hard." When I'm at that point I can then say, "Okay. This is as far as I can go. Now, God, will you help me with the rest? Will you take away any remaining pain that I have now? Will you help?"

That's the other part of co-creation. Now, at the beginning, we may have already been contacting our Higher Power. So it doesn't mean that we have to wait until we've done everything we can do and then involve God. But now, we can turn over any remaining pain to the God of our understanding. A problem with some people in some Twelve-Step programs is that they thought that all they needed to do was to turn it over immediately and then not have to do any work. It goes back to the old Ben Franklin saying, "The Lord helps those who help themselves." That's a basic principle in the process of co-creation. The Twelve Steps are such beautiful examples of using co-creation—as is the Serenity Prayer.*

Q: What does *co-creation* mean here?

A: Co-creation means that I—in concert with the God of my understanding—together, we work through and heal whatever pain and conflicts that might come up for me.

---

*God, grant me the Serenity / to accept the things I cannot change; / Courage to change the things I can; / and Wisdom to know the difference.

Q: So Step Three is not a totally passive Step. It's not simply sitting back and saying, "God, you do everything for me."

A: No. Step Three is not passive at all, because it starts out with "made a decision." It's immediately active. I made that decision and then I turned my life and will over to the care of God. And I'm also tuning in to the God of *my personal* understanding. So this is a very active step. It's not passive.

THE TWELVE STEPS OF ALCOHOLICS ANONYMOUS AND OTHER SELF-HELP FELLOWSHIPS

1. We admitted we were powerless over alcohol [or fill in the blank]—that our lives had become unmanageable.
2. Came to believe that a Power greater than ourselves could restore us to sanity.
3. Made a decision to turn our will and our lives over to the care of God *as we understood Him.*
4. Made a searching and fearless moral inventory of ourselves.
5. Admitted to God, ourselves, and to another human being the exact nature of our wrongs.
6. Were entirely ready to have God remove all these defects of character.
7. Humbly asked Him to remove our shortcomings.
8. Made a list of all persons we had harmed and became willing to make amends to them all.
9. Made direct amends to such people wherever possible, except when to do so would injure them or others.
10. Continued to take personal inventory and when we were wrong promptly admitted it.
11. Sought through prayer and meditation to improve our conscious contract with God *as we understood Him,* praying only for knowledge of His will for us and the power to carry that out.
12. Having had a spiritual awakening as a result of these steps, we tried to carry this message to alcoholics [or others as appropriate] and to practice these principles in all our affairs.

7

The Fourth
and Fifth Steps

Barbara Whitfield: Step Four talks about making a searching and fearless moral inventory of ourselves. Step Five says that we "Admitted to God, to ourselves and to another human being the exact nature of our wrongs." These call for humility and courage. What's the importance of this kind of soul searching and acknowledgment of it, and of the outcome that's involved in the process? Why work these two steps?

Charles Whitfield: Well, these steps first suggest a *moral* inventory. And my understanding of moral is that it means the relationship—the differences and interaction—of good and bad, between strength and weakness. A lot of people leave out, in this inventory, their *strengths*. And so I suggest that when working this step people give as much attention to their strengths as their weaknesses. I believe people are *not born with* these so-called "character defects"—which are the weaknesses. These are *not* necessarily *inherent* in any person. I think these so-called weaknesses come about mostly by two mechanisms. One is by the *wounding* we get when we are little kids growing up in the unhealthy families of trauma in which most of us seem to grow up. That's the first.

The second way to acquire a character defect is by our conditioned *attachment to our false self* or ego. This one is major and takes a lot of work to overcome. Working the steps helps here. Those two situations are what bring about these so-called character defects.

RELATIONSHIP TO CORE ISSUES

These character defects are intimately related to what we call *core issues*, like needing to be in *control*, *all or none* thinking and behaving, difficulty handling *conflict*, fear of *abandonment*, *high tolerance for inappropriate behavior*, difficulty with *feelings*, difficulty being *real*. There are about fifteen or so of these core recovery issues that I describe in my writings and which others have talked about in the recovery field (see pages 62 and 63). These are many of the "defects" that we're talking about in the Fourth Step. These are the "weaknesses," and they are also nearly always the effects of trauma. This simple reframe opens a whole new world to us in working a Fourth and Fifth Step and later, in Stage Two recovery work.

I can't do anything about a problem unless I know what it is. I can't get mastery over anything that I don't first own. So when I name and *own* a character defect, *then* I can begin to heal it. For example, I may own having a weakness like shame (which is not actually a weakness; it's a feeling, and a core issue, that has usually been projected *onto* and *into* me). And so that's why this is such a powerful pair of steps here. And why it takes a lot of courage, because we have to go down underneath what first appears to be on the surface. We've got to go under water. We go into our unconscious. We go into the part of us that we don't want to face. Jung called it "The Shadow." We go down into that darkness and begin to bring it up little by little. That's why recovery takes so long. That's why working this kind of program takes so long. It can't be done in a short time.

Q: Why look at that shadow? Why can't people do something easier and live happily ever after?

A: Addiction and co-dependence are one guise of our shadow. Shadow contains a lot of the unfinished business that we couldn't deal with at the time of the original traumas.

82

We couldn't deal with it for several reasons. That resulting unfinished business is still not complete for us. It's still incomplete. It's going to keep coming up and grabbing hold of us until we attend to it—until we give it attention, appropriate attention—as the illustration in figure 1 shows. That's where recovery comes in and that's where working Steps Four and Five specifically comes in. In working them, we are becoming aware of the shadow—which is coming up as the repetition compulsion (i.e., making the same mistake over and over).

Figure 1. Unfinished Business
Watercolor, ©1989 Tennessee Dixon

This repeated appearance of pain and conflict is really an opportunity for us to take hold of the shadow and see what it's trying to teach or tell us, or how it's trying to assist us. What it's trying to tell us may be, "Hey! There is something incomplete for you here." Recovery is really an opportunity to complete a lot of our unfinished business.

Q: So by controlling the shadow we could break its destructive effects on our lives?

A: Well, to deal with unfinished business, it's most helpful *not* to try to control it, break it down or dynamite it, or to try to cut it off, because then it will just come back and get us another way—with another addiction, attachment or re-enactment. What's important is recognizing it, owning it, working through its duality—the push and pull, the tension of the two ends of the polarity—good and evil, masculine and feminine, light and dark.

We have hundreds of these opposites here. And so as we bring our unconscious stuff up and work with it—we are just wrestling with the opposites. And somehow as we do that and as we tell our story to safe others over and over—we get more familiar with it. The saying that I like to use is, "I can't let go of something until I know it so well, so intimately, until after I have gotten down on the floor and wrestled with it." So, when I get down on the floor and wrestle with something, I really get to know it experientially and intimately. I gradually get to know it well.

One example is the feeling of fear, which a lot of people call by different names and even try to disguise it with names like *anxiety, panic* and *panic disorder,* but really it's fear that we are talking about. We're scared. So before I can let go of fear, I need to know it so well that I know it from top to bottom, beginning to end, by all of its dimensions and permutations. Once I know it well, and I choose to do so, I can consider letting go of it. Why? Because I now know more exactly what it is that I'm letting go of. By bringing stuff up from our unconscious, from our shadow—our unfinished business, our repetition compulsions—we can eventually complete the business around it by getting down on the floor and wrestling with it. By getting to know it so well, we can say, "Ah! Is that what it was trying to tell me? Is that what I needed to learn to do? Okay." Now I'm ready to let go of it.

Q: Do we gain an understanding from doing this work, this wrestling with our conflicts?

A: Yes. This kind of experiential understanding usually means personal evolution and growth. In other words, I move from a lower part of myself, a lower level of consciousness, into a higher one. I move from the physical, which fear is. Fear is a paralyzing physical phenomenon and feeling. When I let go of fear, I can then move higher into my sanity, into my wholeness. I can move from the physical up even through the mental now, and the emotional, and maybe get into and realize the spiritual. What's left when we let go of fear, spiritual masters have suggested, is *Love*. That's not infatuation, and that's not romantic love—but it's Love with a capital L. It's the Love that Higher Power seems to be constantly sending to each of us. The trick, of course, is for us to *open* to God's Love for us. Another word for God's Love-in-action is Holy Spirit.

THE SPIRITUAL BYPASS

Q: Talk about the difference between the emotional and spiritual. Some people might wonder about the difference between emotional growth and spiritual growth.

A: Well, I think the emotional and spiritual intersect. Spiritual is usually of a higher order than emotional. But it doesn't mean that if I can jump up into the spiritual I won't need to deal with my feelings. To get to the spiritual we need to feel and traverse our feelings. For example, I've seen some people who are "born again." By the way, I'm not saying this as derogatory to having that kind of an awakening experience. It can be wonderful. Bill Wilson apparently went through it when he had his white light experience in his final detox at Townes Hospital in New York. That awakening and enlightening experience is great—except that there is a trap inherent within it. There are some people who are born again who will find that it happens so dramatically and so powerfully that they feel as though they go right up into God's arms. They feel God's Love. And then they come back or try to integrate into the rest of the world and they find doing that difficult.

This kind of born-again experience can be difficult for many because they have bypassed an important part of themselves from which they have jumped. They have jumped from the physical or the physical/mental plane right up into the spiritual. People have called that jumping a *spiritual bypass*. Others have called it *premature transcendence* or *high-level denial*. What has been bypassed is the True Self, which is the hub of our being. When we go back and address the True Self, there's where the emotions are. Where the feelings are. So it's important to go back and heal our Child Within when we've had a spiritual awakening—to heal our True Self, because the True Self is the only part of us that can successfully connect to God.

I remember when you wrote your book *Spiritual Awakenings* in which you addressed this subject in some more detail.

Q: Yes. When I did research with people who had near-death experiences, I often saw many of them doing a bypass. The problem here, as you've said, is that we can't hold on to our direct relationship with God if we haven't done our own work on our ego or false self. We had to realize that only our True Self knows God. For people who had a near-death experience and didn't know about recovery (and I'm including my own experience here)—our Twelfth Step strangely or paradoxically happened first.

Many of us would like to believe that we don't need to work on our ego or our false self. We want to believe that in our near-death experience we were healed and we don't need to do any psychological or emotional work. Then, when we miss our *experiential* connection to God enough, we start searching. Even though I did research on near-death studies, my colleagues and I didn't know what the missing component was to help near-death experiencers connect again. Later, when I found out about recovery and the Twelve Steps, I realized I had found the missing component.

A: Please read the Fifth Step again. I wanted to say something more about it.

Q: "Admitted to God, ourselves and another human being the exact nature of our wrongs."

A: This Fifth Step is probably the only one of the Twelve Steps that I question some. I suggest that to admit the exact nature of our *wrongs only* may not be so helpful. I would reconsider that word *wrongs.* Maybe it would be more constructive here to say "the exact nature of our strengths and weaknesses," because if that's all we did in the Fourth Step (i.e. admit only our wrongs), then addressing wrongs only emphasizes the weaknesses instead of also including our strengths. Viewing and working the Fourth and Fifth Steps in this way increases their healing effect.

8

The Sixth
and Seventh Steps

Barbara Whitfield: Step Six says, "Were entirely ready to have God remove all these defects of character." Seven says, "Humbly asked Him to remove our shortcomings." Can we look at the words "defects of character" in the framework of recovery? Also, what are your ideas about asking God to remove our shortcomings, and the important word "humbly," as well?

Charles Whitfield: The Sixth Step is talking about getting ready. It seems like we need to prepare. It takes a while to let go of something and let God. And so this is the *preparation* step. We are *becoming* willing. We are *getting ready*. We are *developing* a little willingness, as *A Course in Miracles* says. More humility. We are getting a more and more open mind. We are getting more and more familiar with exactly what we want to let go. So, while it seems simple (one of the shortest steps of the Twelve), it's still important, and working it might take a long time. It usually does. Many of us don't trust God, since other authority figures have hurt us, didn't protect us, or let us down in some way.

Decades after the Twelve Steps were written (I believe they were written in 1937–1938), psychology researchers Prochaeska and DeClementis have documented the importance of *getting ready* as being a crucial part of the process of change.

Q: Why do people feel reluctant to do a Sixth and Seventh Step? Or why do they gloss over it? Why do people hang on to their defects of character?

A: We tend to hang on to our core issues, these so-called "character defects," because that's what we are most familiar with. It's hard to let go of them—something that we are so familiar with. They probably helped us survive growing up in a troubled family, with a lot of pain. Then later they probably helped us survive parts of our addictions and compulsions. So they've been our friends, too, these so-called "character defects." It's hard to let them go. Also, they are fostered by our false self. That's the hardest "character defect" of all to let go of—our attachment to our false self. We have a strong attachment to it. I think our single greatest addiction is not to alcohol, not to drugs, not to food, work, sex or relationships, but to our false self.

Q: I believe this could be another way you are describing spiritual bypass. Can you say more? What would be an example of being addicted to one's false self?

A: Some of the characteristics of the false self, i.e., our ego, is that it wants to be right, in control, win and survive. It doesn't care how it does it. And it will use all kinds of tactics, both subtle and overt, to try to convince our True Self that it has the answers for us. And since it helped us survive as kids and as adults, we have become quite attached to it. It's hard to let it go. It's also hard to let go of our need to be right all the time, to be in control, to push down all of our feelings, not just painful ones, but joyful feelings too. Those are some of the ways that we can be attached to our false self. And of course, as we move through our recovery and evolve, we get closer and closer to living a life of co-creation. We make the discovery that the false self is not real. It's an illusion. That takes a lot of courage to begin to let go of our false self. To see that and experience it, and know it. And to know that our false self is not God.

Q: Are these character defects or core issues actually ways

which we limit ourselves from realizing who we really are?

A: Well, the character defects or core issues started out as being our friends. They helped us to survive. But when we get closer to healthy relationships, they get in the way. What we are trying to do in recovery, since we're getting into healthier relationships (which is one important aspect of recovery), is that we may want to let go of these various defects. Before we can let go of them, we have to not only be willing, but we have to know what it is that we're letting go of. That's why I have described above the importance of getting down on the floor and wrestling with it before I can know what it is that I am letting go of.

9

The Eighth and Ninth Steps

Barbara Whitfield: Step Eight says, "Made a list of all persons we had harmed and became willing to make amends to them all." And Step Nine says, "Made direct amends to such people wherever possible, except when to do so would injure them or others." Why is that important to make amends to other people? Why do I have to? Why should I go and pay back some money I owe someone or tell somebody that I deeply regret having hurt them, or whatever? Where does that fit into the healing process?

Charles Whitfield: Making amends helps people heal on multiple levels. One is that it allows them to forgive whatever and however the other people were involved. Perhaps, more important, it allows them to hear others, forgive them and say, "Okay. I accept your making amends here. I accept your apology." There's a real healing there. Otherwise people may hold on to resentment, tension and conflict and consequences, which can show up as the repetition compulsion—making the same mistake over and over. Making amends can facilitate a powerful purging of all that has gone on before in working the first seven steps.

Q: What if the other people don't forgive us? If they don't accept our amends?

A: Well, that's why I have suggested to people that as they work each step that they work it with a sponsor or their clergy or some trusted friend or safe person who, by the way, has ideally also *worked through the steps themselves*, so that they know the steps fairly intimately. They can then take that non-forgiveness and work it through, and then work on it some more. It's all grist for the mill. It's more unfinished business. And then, they can eventually discover that it's not the other people, necessarily, who need to forgive them. Rather, they need to forgive themselves for having done it. By working Eight and Nine we are addressing *self*-forgiveness as much as being open to the others' potential forgiveness.

These are the final of the three paired steps (Four and Five, Six and Seven, and now Eight and Nine). And Four through Seven go together, as well. These Twelve Steps are remarkable in their economy and powerful in their concentration, since they contain only 214 words total.

Q: How do these steps work for people who have been victimized? Why should a person who has been a victim make amends? How do you interpret that?

A: I don't see anything useful here in Steps Eight and Nine for people who have been abused. This is because if they go to their abuser and make amends to their abuser they may be asking for more abuse. My sense is that these two steps are more important if I have *harmed another*. If I have hurt another in the past and I want to apologize. This addresses my *guilt* more than my shame.

Q: I understand. Even so, people sometimes feel they have been responsible for having been abused, even when that's not true. How can people guard against making amends for wrongs they feel they may have done, but haven't?

A: Here's where I think it's important to have a safe and experienced person to talk to before doing these steps or at least while doing them. That's why it's useful to get some of the workbooks or work pamphlets that are available for each step (Hazelden published these in the past). These kinds of worksheets and sharing with safe others give a person guidance as they go along here. So talk to your sponsor. Talk to your clergy, your trusted person who is going to maybe give you a little more objective information and perhaps by their mirroring what's really happening. A caution, though, is if they have done a spiritual bypass themselves, they may try to minimize or invalidate the importance of your trauma history.

Q: Can working these steps sometimes help people to understand that they *haven't been responsible* for their having been abused or neglected? For example, with abuse and trauma, people often go through their lives feeling, "It was really my fault and I deserved what I got," when it wasn't. Can doing the steps help them to see that more clearly?

A: I think working the Twelve Steps brings out a whole lot of unknown and undiscovered conflicts, hurt and pain. So if I discover in working the Eighth Step that I really don't need to make amends to somebody who has abused me, because I wasn't really responsible, then that might be a great revelation and in itself part of a great healing.

Q: I've heard you say in your workshops that we're not bad, sick, crazy or stupid, that we are just wounded. In large part we are suffering from the effects of trauma. From what you've just told me, this is one important place where we can find that out. This is where we earn the right to give up all those negative judgments against ourselves. I can give up feeling guilty about something I was punished for when I was four or five years old and I was just trying to escape from having someone inflict terrible pain onto me.

A: That's right! We can now give up those labels that our abusers projected onto us.

10

The Tenth and Eleventh Steps

Barbara Whitfield: Step Ten says, "Continued to take personal inventory and when we were wrong promptly admitted it." But why do I need to keep monitoring myself so carefully? Why can't I just get on—now that I've quit drinking, quit using other drugs, now that I'm out of that relationship, etc., then why can't I just get on with my life?

Charles Whitfield: Focusing enough on my *inner life* is probably the most important thing I can do in early recovery, because by doing so, I get to know an important part of me that I might have pushed away (see Figure 10.1). Now, as my recovery proceeds, I also have to pay attention to my outer life and get this balance. So what I do by practicing the Tenth Step is that I continue taking this inventory, continuing to focus on what's happening in my inner life. In other words, when I have hurt someone, when I've made a mistake, when I've done something that was against my values, then I can bring it into my awareness and own it—admit it, process it, and if it was painful, then let it go.

When I own something, it loses its power over me. For instance, if I'm angry, but I pretend that I'm not angry—it's got power over me. And it's going to work on me until something happens. If I *claim* that anger and say, "Yes. I am angry. This is anger that I'm feeling in my guts, in my inner life right now. And it's about something. It's telling me something important." Of course, my anger may also not be telling me anything, or it may be misleading me which happens often. It depends. That's why "the wisdom to know the difference" is so important here. As I own it, I can use it, and

I can also choose to let go of it if I want. So I think the Tenth Step involves this ongoing self-reflection in a healthy way that's very important to the total process of recovery.

A maintenance step, the Tenth Step is also important by its helping us keep our powerful humility, which helps us stay open to what is real in our relationship with our self, others and God. Working it also helps us let go of our attachment to our ego in an ongoing way.

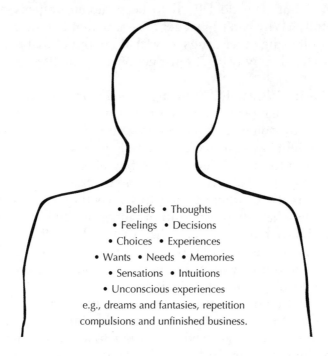

- Beliefs • Thoughts
- Feelings • Decisions
- Choices • Experiences
- Wants • Needs • Memories
- Sensations • Intuitions
- Unconscious experiences
e.g., dreams and fantasies, repetition
compulsions and unfinished business.

Figure 10.1. My Inner Life

Q: What about the Eleventh Step: "Sought through prayer and meditation to improve our conscious contact with God . . . praying only for knowledge of His will for us and the power to carry that out." We often hear these Twelve-Step programs described as *spiritual* rather than *religious*. There's a lot of interest in God and prayer and meditation now. Talk about what *spiritual* rather than *religious* means. Some people think these are religious programs.

A: Well, religious to me implies a more limited attempt at understanding our wholeness and our relationship with self, others and God. Spirituality is a more expanded way of viewing and understanding those key relationships. Spirituality is not limited to any one faith. It doesn't say you have to know your Buddha Nature. Buddha Nature may be an important thing to know because it's the same in the Western world as "Christ Consciousness." And those are crucial understandings. Nonetheless, of the clergy and others who work in the various religious faiths, every one of them has a false self. They all have an ego that gets in the way and starts scrambling things up. How can there be more than one God? The powerful scriptures say "The Lord is One." So, spirituality brings us back into a much more expanded sense of self, others and God, while at the same time it doesn't reject religion. It's not anti-religious by any means, as some fundamentalists might want to believe—as they cling to their own egos. But spirituality includes, supports and nurtures religion—all the religions—while at the same time it *transcends* them.

I have a question for you. I've heard you say many times, "Religions are brand names. Spirituality is the generic." Spirituality is the umbrella that includes all religions and transcends them to a direct relationship with God/Goddess/All-That-Is. What about that?

Q: Yes. That is what I realized when I interviewed near-death experiencers. And, spirituality is completely

99

compatible with religion, and at the same time it transcends it. That's so important for us to realize. We can continue practicing our religion if we so choose, but we can also have our own personal and direct experience of Spirit with a capital S. This is a direct experience that fills us in a way that our addictions could never do. That emptiness we were trying to fill with chemicals or people, etc., could never fulfill us like an ongoing direct experience of God. Spirituality also includes our relationship with our self, our Child Within. When we realize that relationship, we then can maintain that direct relationship with God in a more fulfilling way.

THE MEANING OF GOD'S WILL

Q: What does the Eleventh Step mean to you when it talks about "praying only for knowledge of [God's] will for us and the power to carry that out"? What does concern for God's will mean in the framework of recovery?

A: The Eleventh is the longest in words of the Twelve Steps. It's got a lot of action. And I think we could spend a whole week talking about just this step, because it has several key words. One of them, again, is *will*. We go back to that word from the Third Step—*What is God's will for us?* So we are praying and meditating—we are seeking through prayer and meditation to find out what is God's will for us—and we ask for the power to carry out that will. It's a Divine Mystery. The whole thing is a mystery. However, we can begin to consider that maybe what God's will for us is what the Second Step has addressed, and that word is *sanity,* which is also *wholeness*. God's will for us is to be whole—to be physical, mental, emotional and spiritual beings and to have this *human experience* as spiritual beings—and to have what we in the recovery field call *serenity*—to realize serenity. *A Course in Miracles* calls this *complete peace and joy.*

100

And, finally, perhaps God's will for us is to be creative—to be co-creative with the God of our understanding. So we are seeking through prayer and meditation these powerful spiritual practices, which I think people are getting into more now. I think meditation is just beginning to be tapped, because meditation when we are alone is powerful. And meditation done in a group at least once a week is even more powerful in realizing our self and God. So I think more people in recovery are going to be considering prayer and meditation in their spiritual practices. So, we are seeking through these two powerful spiritual practices the knowledge of God's will for us, the Knowledge, I would say not with just a small k, but with a capital K, and then the power to carry that out. That is an unseen force and energy that's coming into us as we pray, meditate and thereby realize self and God.

11

The Twelfth Step

Barbara Whitfield: Step Twelve talks about a *spiritual awakening.* It says, "Having had a spiritual awakening as the result of these steps, we tried to carry this message to alcoholics, and to practice these principles in all our affairs." What is a spiritual awakening in the framework of these steps?

Charles Whitfield: Rather than a single spiritual awakening, I would say it was more accurately *several* or a *series* of awakenings. These are psycho-spiritual in nature. I've asked a lot of people and they say, "Yeah. This has happened to me." Check it out with yourself. Have you ever been going along in your ordinary day-to-day life, your ordinary waking consciousness, and for a second something clicked in and you said "This is not real!" (i.e., my ordinary earthly view of my life right now). Has that ever happened to you? I think it has happened to a lot of people, maybe most people. And I think that's an example of one possibility for spiritual awakening— right there. When we allow that to go on into seconds or minutes, we can then have a more authentic, successful spiritual awakening. When we allow our perception to open to what is happening, when we pause with this little miracle, when we stop rushing through life. And we pause, as this moment of spiritual awakening changes our perception of everything, including time. This is because time stops if we become still enough to slip into this space between this reality and God's. These kinds of experiences are often trying to break through for us.

Q: That's why you believe prayer and meditation are so important. By practicing them, we are actually making time and space for these spiritual awakenings, and in recovery it helps to have a series of these awakenings.

A: Yes. And the words "having had a spiritual awakening" could be translated more accurately as "having had a series of spiritual awakenings." Those awakenings are to self and God—to the experience of the Understanding (with a capital U) of self and God. And, of course, as we understand self and God more, we can then understand others more. We have this three-part relationship here—self, others and God. So in the Twelfth Step, here we are, having had this awakening—this psycho-spiritual awakening, self-awareness, God awareness, God consciousness—and knowing how others have helped us heal.

Working the Twelfth Step I then take that message to others. However, there are a couple of catches here. And one of them has to do with the important spiritual principles and practices of *humility* and *compassion*—that I cannot be grandiose when I am bringing my spiritual awareness and my assistance to another person. I have to remain humble. So compassionate people are humble. They are open. They are still open to learning about self, others and God, which to me is one basic definition of *humility*.

I come in with that compassion, which also means that I'm not attached to the outcome of this particular contact with this person I'm trying to assist. If they choose not to listen or if they choose not to do what I'm modeling or suggesting, or whatever, then I let go of it. I'm not attached, addicted or clinging to it. One of the ways I can help with that is by always bringing another person with me. So AA suggests never to make a Twelfth-Step call, an intervention, without being accompanied by another person who is in the program. In other areas of my life, if I don't have another person, I always have my Higher Power. Or I can always also go back to other safe and trusted people like my sponsor, my best friend, maybe my partner, my whomever, and share that with them.

PREVENTING RELAPSE

Q: Going a little beyond the steps, what is the best way to avoid relapse?

A: I think the best way to avoid relapse is to continue working a full recovery program in whatever stage of recovery I may be in. So, if I'm in Stage One recovery, that is addressing my addictions or other disorders, then I do that. And I've described this in my writings and other people have also in theirs. Stage Two recovery is trauma-focused recovery. So, I do that work. That is also helpful in relapse prevention. As a matter of fact, all the people that used to relapse a couple of decades ago and beyond, when they were relapsing we thought there was something constitutionally wrong with them. As a matter of fact, it says that in the first paragraph of chapter 5 of "The Big Book" of AA—that these people might be constitutionally defective and they're kind of hopeless. The whole adult-child, co-dependence and trauma-survivor movement has corrected that and said, "No, most people are not constitutionally defective in this way, and they can work a program as an Adult Child of trauma and begin to correct those 'character defects' even more." In that way, they can help prevent relapse. And finally, in Stage Three recovery, I can continue on my spiritual journey and spiritual practices of my choice and slowly learn what God's will is for me, which, it seems, is to be a co-creator of my life.

A COURSE IN MIRACLES

Q: I know that some people in recovery are studying *A Course in Miracles*. Do any of its teachings help in understanding spirituality? And is the Course's message similar to that of the Twelve Steps?

A: The Course has been a help to many spiritual seekers.

I've known a fair number of people recovering in Twelve-Step programs who have found spiritual nourishment by studying the Course. One example is how it sees *resentments*. Twelve-Step fellowships, such as Alcoholics Anonymous and others, speak of what the modern holy book, *A Course in Miracles*, calls "special relationships" in various ways. One to consider is the trap that we all seem to get into called resentments. Almost by definition, when we have a resentment toward any person, place or thing, we are most likely to be enmeshed in that kind of a special relationship. Not wanting to tolerate the emotional pain of the resentment, and not knowing what to do to heal it, we often search out our drug or behavior of choice to lessen the associated pain. And our ego, which AA calls "King Baby" at its extreme, is probably our biggest addiction or attachment. Over and over, the ego has caused us a lot of pain. But the Course says that there is a better way to handle our pain and eventually get some peace.

I believe that the message of the Course is quite compatible with the Twelve Steps. It compliments and expands them in a positive way.

It says that whenever we may find ourselves involved in a painful or conflicted relationship, we can remember that, as with any pain or conflict, we always have a choice. Whenever we are not at peace, we can remember that we are *attached* to or are *in* our ego. To be at peace, we can pray to God, simply asking for help. We can choose God, and then surrender to "let go and let God," into God's love and peace. It is that simple. Yet, it is complex, too, since our ego constantly tries to disrupt and complicate our peace. The Course is the best antidote to ego attachment that I have ever found.

Since more and more people in recovery are studying the Course, I have put together a table to show how similar some of the key terms are in each of these spiritual paths. By the way, the Course is not an actual course that we can take somewhere. Rather, it's a book for self-study that has been spiritually nourishing for a lot of people.

Table 6. Similarity of Selected Terms from Twelve-Step Work and *A Course in Miracles*

Alcoholics Anonymous Terms	*A Course in Miracles* Terms
Step 2.* Sanity	Right mindedness, seeing with Christ's vision
3. Decision (Made a . . .)	Decision maker, choice maker (a part of our "right mind")
4. Moral inventory	Ego undoing, forgiveness process
5. 6. & 7. Our wrongs, character defects, shortcomings	Ego attachment, wrong mind, mistakes
7. Humbly asked (humility)	Humility, openness, willingness
8. & 9. Making amends	Let go of ego/forgive
10. Continuing to take personal inventory	Vigilance for ego
11. Prayer & meditation	Prayer, miracles
Serenity	Inner peace

* Number of step of AA and other self-help fellowships.

MORE THAN OUR BODY

Q: I interviewed several subjects in our research into near-death experiences that spoke about being out of their bodies during incest or rape. We know now that strong physical or emotional pain can trigger an out-of-body experience (OBE) and possibly more stages of the near-death experience.*

To me this is another example of when the Twelfth Step happens first. Some of these people had already joined Twelve-Step programs and others didn't know about them, but needed to connect. They considered their OBEs to be miracles. Some said "divine intervention" rescued them, even though they knew it was logically impossible. They said it was those miracles that kept them alive despite lives full of injury and pain. Some of them described elaborate experiences that contained many of the stages of a near-death experience.

A man who was abused as a child and has PTSD recently told me, "I try to remember that these experiences and the miracles that I have witnessed are real. In our culture, where logic is the only legitimate way of thinking, and where money is the ultimate value that confers value on everything else, it is easy to forget that there is a metaphysical realm that is as real, if not more so, than the physical. It also seems to me that medicine and the human sciences have tended to focus on a mechanistic view of human life at the expense of the

---

*Many "old 'paradigm'" clinicians would interpret these descriptions of leaving the body as dissociation. My colleagues from the University of Connecticut, Kenneth Ring and Richard Rosing, discussed this in detail in their paper *The Omega Project* where they studied seventy-four near-death experiencers and fifty-four persons who were interested in near-death experiences but had never had one (control group). The purpose of this survey was to assess the role of psychological and developmental factors in influencing susceptibility to near-death experiences (NDEs) or alternate realities. In summarizing, they said, "[What is] the core defining feature of the NDE-prone personality? In our judgment, it is the capacity to shift into states of consciousness that afford access to alternative or non-ordinary realities coupled with strong tendencies toward psychological absorption. That is, the person who is especially likely to register and recall an NDE is one whose awareness is easily able to transcend the sensory world and enter into focused attention to interior states. Once the shift to non-sensory realities has occurred, it seems to be the capacity for psychological absorption that is crucial."

spiritual. In that sense, the spiritual may be a person's only true possession."

A: I'm glad you brought that up. Many people in recovery have had experiences that have shown them that they are more than just their physical body. But because of the limited ways we have been taught or programmed about religion and the spiritual, we learn to discount or repress some of our transcendent experiences. We can talk about our direct experiences in recovery. As we do so, we may experientially remember and know that we are more than our bodies. Whether triggered by physical or emotional pain or near-death, these experiences can show us that we are spiritual beings inhabiting a physical body.

Q: It has been said that the recovery process is not something that gets done, and then it is finished and over with. Can you talk about this?

A: Well, I think we can get this to be 70 or 80 or 90 percent completed, and then we can sit back and relax a lot more. But the Universe keeps handing us things. Our unfinished business keeps coming. So we deal with it as it comes up. That's why it's important to continue with spiritual practices—continue with some kind of self-examination and awareness and psycho-spiritual work—which is also important for ongoing relapse prevention.

Q: So our recovery and our life goes on, but now we have tools—skills to deal with whatever comes up. And at the same time, we now better understand the difference between catastrophizing and realistically looking at a problem or conflict. A trauma survivor once told us that before recovery, if he had a flat tire on his car, he would feel like he wanted to call the suicide hotline. Now he reacts like he needs to call AAA.

The Twelve Steps are so successful. Why do they prolifer-ate—obviously from AA more than sixty years ago, and they have spread. They've been adapted for use by a multitude of people dealing with a multitude of problems. Why are they so appealing to so many people?

A: I think the basic reason that the Twelve Steps are so appealing is because they work. They help people and they are a great guidepost and assistance on people's journey of life and recovery.

Q: In your experience working with people and as a medi-cal doctor, can you tell us your assessment of and the value and potential effectiveness of using the Twelve Steps?

A: As a physician and therapist, assisting people as they heal, I think learning about the Twelve Steps and learning about the spiritual, which are both part of the new paradigm in human well-being and in the helping professions, has been the greatest single aid that I have found for helping people with all kinds of disorders and conditions.

To me, working the Twelve Steps are not only often diffi-cult at the start, but eventually they are fun. Not only do they work to help us heal when we work them, but often during our working of them, and certainly at the end, we can feel some real enjoyment and peace in our life.

12

Stage Three Recovery:

Spirituality

A goal of Stage Three recovery is learning to live in the present moment and realizing a healthy and nourishing spirituality. No longer burdened by the past or fearing the future, I become able to live in what spiritual seekers call "the eternal now."

A side effect or result of working a recovery program, of living in the now and of regular spiritual practice, is serenity. Serenity is also called by many other names, including enlightenment, nirvana, samadhi and God consciousness.

There may be other goals and results, including having no goals and expecting no results. The third Zen patriarch said, "The Great Way is not difficult for those who have no preferences."

But before entering Stage Three recovery, it can be useful for me to check whether I have worked through recovery Stages One and Two sufficiently, so that I will be more likely to benefit from working a Stage Three recovery program. I show a summary of these stages in Table 7.

REVIEW OF RECOVERY

Let's look at the map of recovery (Table 7). This map reads from bottom to top.

When to focus on Stages Two and Three recovery usually depends upon the person's prior healing and present condition.

STAGE ZERO

Stage Zero is manifested by the presence of any active illness, such as an addiction, compulsion or other disorder.

These disorders may be physical, mental, emotional or spiritual. I described some of them briefly in my recovery plan for Stage One. This active illness may be acute, recurring or chronic. Without recovery, it may continue indefinitely. At Stage Zero, recovery hasn't yet started.

When to focus on Stages Two and Three recovery usually depends upon the person's prior healing and present condition.

Table 7. Recovery & Duration According to Stages

Recovery Stage	Condition	Focus of Recovery	Approximate Duration
3	Human/ spiritual	Spirituality	Ongoing
2	Trauma effects	Trauma-specific full recovery program	3 to 5 years
1	Stage Zero disorder	Basic-illness specific full recovery program	½ to 3 years
0	Active illness	Addiction, compulsion or disorder	Indefinite
		------------------------ Woundedness, trauma effects	

STAGE ONE

At Stage One, recovery begins. It involves participating in a full recovery program for whatever condition (Stage Zero) that I might have. This Stage One full recovery program assists me in healing any Stage Zero disorder or condition that I might have.*

STAGE TWO

Having a stable and solid Stage One recovery—one that has lasted for at least a year or longer—it may be time to consider looking into our Adult Child or childhood trauma issues, which is Stage Two recovery. "Adult Child" is a term that helps us better understand the experience of anyone who grew up in an unhealthy, troubled or dysfunctional family. Many Adult Children may still be in a similar unhealthy environment, whether at home, in one or more relationships, and/or at their workplace.

One major manifestation of these trauma effects is co-dependence. My briefest definition of co-dependence is that it is any suffering and dysfunction associated with focusing on the needs and behavior of others. It is outer focusing to the detriment of self. As a primary effect of trauma it usually underlies any and all of the addictions, compulsions and other disorders that I have briefly defined in chapter 2.

While the Adult Child syndrome and co-dependence do not cause most Stage Zero conditions, they do regularly aggravate them and often contribute to their relapse. This Adult Child condition and co-dependence are caused by a wounding, which results in often painful effects that cover the physical, mental, emotional and spiritual aspects of our being and life.**

By working the most complete full recovery program, Stage Two recovery usually takes from three to five years to accomplish. For some people, it may take longer. There is absolutely no rush or need to hurry this part of recovery. I can take as long as I need, and to assist me I can refer to chapter 4.

One way to know that I have not yet completed Stage Two

---

*I describe the process of Stage One recovery in chapter 14 of *A Gift to Myself* and chapter 10 of *Co-Dependence*, as well as in chapter 2 of this book.

**I describe this wounding in *Healing the Child Within*, *A Gift to Myself*, *Co-Dependence* and *The Truth about Depression*.

recovery is when I cannot experience peace and serenity while working a Stage Three recovery program.

STAGE THREE

Stage Three recovery is about realizing a progressively richer and deeper spirituality. You may have already begun to incorporate it into your life during your work in any stage of recovery. This chapter is about Stage Three recovery, which is about spirituality.

As you read this chapter, keep in mind what blocks, problems, issues or concerns that you might have in realizing a fulfilling spirituality in your life. Write these down or mark them, so that at the end you will be able to list them as a part of your personal Recovery Plan.

BLOCKS TO REALIZING
SPIRITUALITY AND SERENITY

Spirituality is a powerful healing force in all three recovery stages. Yet many of us have a hard time making it work for us. To what might that be due? I have identified at least twelve blocks over which we can stumble on our healing journey to realizing spirituality and serenity.

1. *We don't know what spirituality is.* We can start by saying that spirituality is about our relationships with our self, others and our Higher Power. It expands in proportion to our awareness of our inner life (which we learn in Stage Two recovery) and our personal and experiential relationships with these three. If convenient, I suggest reading chapter 15, The Role of

114

Spirituality, in *Healing the Child Within*. If interested in more, read *Emmanuel's Book II*.

2. *We confuse spirituality with organized religion.* While it includes, nurtures and supports organized religion, as it does most everything that is positive in the universe, spirituality transcends organized religion. It is far deeper and richer.

3. *We associate Higher Power with parents, like our father, mother or other figures.* Could it be that we project or transfer onto our Higher Power much of our resentment and other unfinished business with our parents? If we do, we may project . . .

4. *Resentment at our Higher Power.* Some reasons may include that we believe God has punished us for being bad or that we are angry with God for sending us into such a troubled family and life. Related to all this, we may also . . .

5. *Have negative, preconceived notions of Higher Power, e.g., an angry or unavailable One.* We may have been taught this by authority figures, including some biblical and religious writers and clergy who themselves may have been or are still unhealed Adult Children of trauma projecting these notions onto their Higher Power and onto us.

6. *I may be unaware of who I really am, i.e., my True Self, my Child Within.* Identifying with my false or co-dependent self, I may not be aware of my integrity, wholeness and sanity as the Second Step addresses. This unawareness may be related to the fact that we . . .

7. *Have not healed our Child Within,* i.e., have not done our basic Adult Child recovery work in a Stage Two full recovery program. This may also include not having done basic Stage One recovery work, including working the Twelve Steps. Or we may be . . .

8. *Stuck in the martyr/victim stance or cycle.** We may be able to feel only painful feelings or numbness, and not be aware of our inner life and how we can enter and flow through our Hero/Heroine's Journey. No matter which stage we may be in, our Hero/Heroine's Journey is the journey of recovery. All of the material, techniques and skills that I describe in my writings, and that you can read in others, describe this process. Another block may be that we . . .
9. *Won't take responsibility for our life.* Related to many of the above blocks, we may use this block because we are just accustomed or even addicted to believing and acting as though we can't make our life work. We may not know that we can stop blaming others and the universe, and that we can take responsibility for making an enjoyable success out of our life. We may also be using . . .
10. *No, or ineffective, spiritual practices.* This one and many of the above blocks may also be associated with our having had . . .
11. *No joyful spiritual experiences.* We may also be . . .
12. *Unaware of our co-creatorship with our Higher Power.* Co-creatorship means that in concert with our Higher Power, we take responsibility for creating success and joy in our life.

Many colleagues and I believe that all of these blocks are aggravated by the conventional Judeo-Christian-Islamic ethic with all its trappings of guilt, shame and fear, and by conventional psychology and our conventional physical and mental health delivery systems.

But there is a way out—and that is to heal our Child Within

---

*The martyr/victim cycle is explained on pages 96 through 99 in *Healing the Child Within* and pages 42 and 43 of *Co-Dependence*. Lazaris describes it in more detail on the tape "The Crisis of Martyrhood."

i.e, our True Self (Stage Two recovery), and to continue to work a long-term recovery program that includes an increasing spiritual awareness (Stage Three recovery).

Can you identify with any of the above blocks? If so, would you be interested in making a plan to get free of each one? Use the space below to begin exploring your plan.

_____

_____

_____

_____

_____

_____

_____

_____

_____

_____

_____

We can now begin to summarize our healing journey, which may occur sequentially along the following twelve levels or stages.

This journey is usually more circular than the linear one described in Table 8 on the following page. This is because we can "cycle through it" at any time in the course of our daily, weekly and monthly life. By recognizing just where we are according to these levels, we can focus on that level, consciously work through any conflict around that level, then move on to the next. Using the principles described here and in references at the back of this book can facilitate that work.

Table 8. The Child Within's Psycho-Spiritual Journey

	Corresponding Recovery Stage
Adult child wounding (original traumas)	
↓	
Emptiness (loss of our True Self)	
↓	
Attempts to fill the emptiness (through co-dependence, addictions and compulsions)	0
↓	
Frustration at looking for fulfillment outside of us	1
↓	
Heal our Child Within, which includes and results in—	2
Healthy boundaries	
↓	
Self-knowledge and authentic life experience	3
↓	
Personal experience of Higher Power	
Connect Child (True Self) with Higher Power	
↓	
Co-creatorship	
↓	
Accept what cannot change; change what can	
↓	
Peace and Serenity	

I believe that once we heal our Child Within and experientially connect it to the God of our understanding, we will experience our spirituality and serenity automatically and naturally. This is because our True Self is the only part of us that is real and that can know our self, others and God authentically.

THE SPIRITUAL BYPASS

In recovery, there is often a temptation to try to move quickly from the early levels or stages to the more advanced ones. We would like to jump from the pain and confusion of our emptiness and our frustration directly into feeling peace and serenity, and thereby bypass the middle stages. (We can call this a pink cloud or a kind of pseudoserenity.) We may be in Stages Zero or One, and for one reason or another, including that it can feel so good to "hang out" with God, we bypass Stage Two recovery. But when we do that, we abandon our True Self, our Child Within, and thereby all of our power, creativity and rich experience.

We can call that jumping or bypassing a "spiritual bypass," "premature transcendence" or "high level denial." It can occur in many situations, such as participating in cults, born-again experiences, guru addiction, by using all sorts of methods and jumping too fast into advanced spiritual techniques and paths.* In short, even otherwise authentic spiritual experiences can at times distract us from living as our True Self. Spiritual seeking and practice can itself at times become a trap. Being a successful human being requires a delicate balance and an integration of all of our levels of consciousness, awareness or being. These include the physical, mental, emotional and spiritual. As described in the Twelve Steps, that is sanity.

---

* See cautions to some of these methods in *A Gift to Myself* on pages 133, 165 and 223.

WHO AM I?

Throughout time, we have often asked ourselves this question. As we process through our own personal healing and recovery we can explore and consider many possible answers. By the time we reach Stage Three recovery, we may begin to come to some conclusions. So—just who am I?

While "the map is not the territory," maps are useful. In helping myself in my own life and the people that I assist in theirs, I have found one particular "map of the mind" to be most useful. In 1990, after reviewing more than 100 other maps of the mind for the past fifteen years, I developed this one. See if any of it may be useful for you.

This map shows that we come from Spirit, our Higher Power. We are each a Child of God—in a healthy dependent relationship with that One. This is our Real, True Self or Child Within. (This part of us has also been called our Existential Self, Heart, Soul or True Identity.) And we each also have a Divine or Higher Self, which some call our "Guardian Angel," Buddha Nature, Atman or Christ-consciousness.

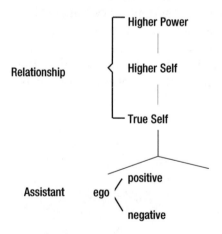

**Figure 3. Map of Healthy Relationships
with Self and Higher Power**

120

We are thus in a healthy relationship with our self, Higher Self and Higher Power or God. Since this relationship is so important and powerful, I like to view it as being one relationship or even one person—a "Sacred Person." It takes a long time to discover and remember this relationship, but it seems to be worth the journey.

And as we journey, our false self or ego can assist us directly as positive ego, or indirectly (and thus with pain and confusion) as negative ego, false or co-dependent self.

Over the past 2,500 years, spiritual teachers and their writings have told us that we have only one enemy—our ego, ego-mind, our false or co-dependent self. Thus, a major task on our spiritual path appears to be to learn to tell the difference between our True Self, with its felt connection to the God of our understanding, and our ego. Making that differentiation experientially has been a major goal of Stage Two recovery, and it is likewise an ongoing goal in Stage Three.*

In Stage Two recovery, I worked on this goal in part by struggling with the pain of risking being my Real Self, getting my healthy human needs met and working through my core recovery issues. To accomplish these, I had to get to know all of them experientially and intimately, a part of which I like to call "getting down on the floor and wrestling with it," e.g., with the pain and the struggle involved in each of these. It is only when I thus come to know such a painful feeling or issue so *authentically* and *completely*, that I can then let go of it, if I choose.

Another word for this letting go is forgiveness. Have you noticed that it is hard to forgive, to let go of something when you are not experientially clear as to exactly what it is you are

---

*For some details on how to differentiate the True Self from the false self, see *Healing the Child Within* on pages 9–12, *A Gift to Myself* on pages 19–23, *Co-Dependence* on pages 241–245, or *Boundaries and Relationships* on pages 204–205.

letting go of? That is why before I can let go of something—
before I can forgive—I have to know experientially and thor-
oughly what it is that I am letting go of. To do that, I have to
work through it, which may take me a long time.

And, even in Stage Three, I will still be working through
my upsets, problems or issues. Only now I will be doing so
with progressively more awareness or consciousness of my
inner life (which I began to learn well in Stage Two recovery
see Figure 10.1). I will now also be able to work through my
problems or upsets more efficiently and successfully. And so,
with the assistance of my Higher Power, I am more and more
focusing on what is real and what is not real. In its introduc-
tion, *A Course in Miracles* says:

> What is real cannot be threatened.
> What is unreal does not exist.
> Herein lies the peace of God.

To me, God and God's world is Real, which is the same as
the world of the Sacred Person, since therein I choose God.
The Course calls this choice "Right Mind." The ego or false
self and its world are unreal and, therefore, do not ultimately
exist. The Course calls choosing the ego's world "wrong
mind." Knowing this in my heart and making the choice for
God in each moment of NOW gives me peace.

In addition to "Who am I?" there may be two more questions. These are "What am I doing here?" and "Where am I
going?" As we journey along our path, we may also begin to
answer these. Regular (ideally daily) spiritual practice can
help us answer all three of these questions—and more.

SPIRITUAL PRACTICE

Spiritual practice is anything I may do regularly that helps
me to get in touch in an experiential way with my Sacred
Person: my True Self, Higher Self and my Higher Power. In

fact, what it tends to do first is to help me get in touch with my True Self. And once I have done that, the regular spiritual practice then tends to assist me in having a heartfelt experience of my Higher Self and Higher Power—the God of my understanding.

I say "of my understanding" because it is my personal and clinical experience that we each have to find our Higher Power in our own way and in our own time. When others may try to tell us how to know God, it usually does not work. That is why many people can become discouraged with conventional organized religion.

But spirituality is not about religion. To start with, it is about our relationships with our self, others and our Higher Power. While spirituality includes, supports and nurtures healthy religion, it also transcends it. Spirituality is personal, thus the term "God of my understanding." And regular spiritual practice can allow me to better know that Higher Power.

Spiritual practice may consist of almost anything that I may do with God-mindedness, while living from and as my True Self. Below I will mention three kinds of spiritual practice that can be helpful. These include meditation, prayer and reading spiritual literature.

Meditation and prayer, when practiced daily and regularly, can be powerful balances and integrators of our whole personality and being. They can help us realize and experience the sanity, the wholeness that the Second of the Twelve Steps addresses. There are numerous books on meditation and prayer, and both are suggested in the Eleventh Step.

MEDITATING

One does not have to be at all interested in religion or even spirituality to learn to meditate effectively. There are several different types of meditation. It is most useful to locate meditation teachers and learn from them, while reading a book or two that they might recommend. If you can't find a teacher and if you have some free time, you might consider the following:

Find a quiet, comfortable place where you will not be interrupted for about an hour. It is best not to have eaten for at least two hours and not to have used any psychoactive drugs or heavy amounts of sugar or sweets for several days. Drugs, including alcohol, nicotine, caffeine and sugar, tend to block a healthy meditation response.

Sit in a comfortable straight-backed chair or on a pillow or meditation bench. Whenever you are ready, begin to quiet your mind and to open your heart. Let your eyes close and take in a deep breath. Then slowly let the breath out. Repeat several times. After you have begun to quiet yourself in this way, say the following two words out loud, clearly . . .

I AM

Then repeat them in a somewhat softer voice and keep repeating I AM until it is just a whisper. Finally repeat it every few seconds in your mind only. If distracting thoughts come in, just watch them as they come and as they go. There is no need to be in control. Just begin to let go and keep repeating the I AM. Somewhere along your way you may notice a mild altered state of consciousness. This is usually an indication of beginning healing and moving toward Wholeness or Sanity.

This is meditation.

Continue meditating for about twenty minutes, then when you are ready, slowly open your eyes. Meditation is safe and it will not interfere with any recovery, counseling or religion. In fact, meditation is most likely to enhance and enrich all aspects of our psycho-spiritual well-being. It can have an immediate effect of helping you experience increased relaxation and energy. Its longer-term effects, which may take years, include a progressively increasing awareness of self, others and the Universe. Often serenity and a sense of peace will begin to appear. To realize these results takes regular practice and a lot of patience.

An ideal program would be to meditate twice daily alone and once weekly in a meditation group.

PRAYING

Similar to meditation, prayer can also be healing. But it takes the same practice and patience. How do we listen and talk to our Higher Power, to something that is so mysterious, powerful and pervasive that we often have difficulty even conceiving of it? A person can pray at any time, needing no special physical posture, paraphernalia, house of worship or ceremony. While it can be helpful to close one's eyes and take a few slow and deep breaths to get into a higher state of consciousness to facilitate praying, even that is not necessary.

What is more important is our "state of heart." Perhaps the only "requirements" for effective prayer are faith, surrender or true humility, and a loving attitude to God and our fellow creatures—states of being which are often difficult to reach.

A spiritual teacher said, "Behold, I stand at the door and knock. If any one hears my voice and opens the door, I will come in to them, and sup with them and they with me." (Christ, Rev. 3:20) It is thus not we who move us to pray, but our Higher Power, perhaps through our Higher Self, Buddha Nature or Christ-Consciousness, which invites us and moves us. Even if we do not have the above "requirements" for prayer, we can still pray in any way we choose that will open ourselves to Universal Consciousness. Whatever comes—whether it be struggle, resistance or frustration, or joy and peace—we can experience it. If we continue to pray with patience and trust, the "required" humility, love and faith will come.

Prayer and meditation are the breath of the Self, with each respiration transferring the radiant and healing energy from Universal Consciousness into us. When we release ourselves, when we totally relax and surrender into the radiant energy of our Higher Power, we begin for the first time to practice with the basic experience and feeling, as well as the intuitive understanding that all living things and beings are already only direct manifestations of Universal Consciousness. We are connected. Our fear and suffering are gone. We are One.

READING AND CONTEMPLATING SPIRITUAL LITERATURE

No matter what religious faith a person may identify with, the available spiritual literature in each is almost endless. And for a person who does not subscribe to a particular religion or faith, there is also an almost endless list of nonsectarian readings.

These readings may include holy books, commentaries on holy books, and other writings. To me, spiritual literature includes almost any writing that nourishes me. When I read it and contemplate it, I feel nourished. With this in mind, many basic recovery books, such as the Big Book of Alcoholics Anonymous and its equivalent from other Twelve-Step fellowships, depending on how they are used, are holy books.

While the list of nourishing books is long and personal, I have found several to be especially helpful for nonsectarian readers. Some of these include *Life of the Beloved, Emmanuel's Book II: The Choice for Love, A Course in Miracles* and any of the writings of White Eagle. The first two and White Eagle's writings are short, simple and easy reading. *A Course in Miracles* is long, both simple and complex, and a person can spend nearly a lifetime studying and being nourished by it. I have also found it particularly useful to "read" the Course by listening to it on tape in my car.

If you already do or would like to read some spiritual literature regularly or irregularly as a spiritual practice, below is some space where you can write their titles.

_____

_____

_____

_____

_____

_____

OUR OBSERVER SELF

One helpful result of regular spiritual practice is learning to live as our "observer self."

As we evolve and grow in our recovery, we discover that there is a part of us, perhaps located somewhere in the higher realms of our True Self, that is able to step back and to watch, witness or observe what is happening in our life. For example, many people have experienced becoming extremely upset, then detaching from their upset and feelings to such an extent that they find themselves actually observing themselves in the upset. Sometimes there is an out-of-body experience, so that they are able to see themselves or a representation of themselves having the upset. This ability can be facilitated by practicing guided imagery and visualizations. Closing the eyes, the person visualizes or otherwise imagines the scene or activity about which there is a concern. One can then visualize a positive solution to the upset. This can also be done while meditating. Done constructively, this is a healthy practice.

Deikman and others call this powerful and freeing part of us the *observer* or *observing self.* The observing self is central to our recovery. An illustration is shown in Figure 4. This shows the interrelationships of the self and the observing self. The self is concerned with thinking, feeling, acting, desiring and other survival-oriented activities. (This older and less useful concept of the self includes parts of both the false self and the True Self.) However, the observer self, a part of who we really are, is that part of us that is watching both our false self and our True Self. We might say that it even watches us when we watch.

It is our Consciousness. It is a core experience of our Real Self. Thus it cannot be watched—at least not by any thing or any being that we know of on this Earth. It transcends our five senses, our co-dependent self and all other lower, though necessary, parts of us.

Some people may confuse their observer self with a kind of defense they may have used to avoid their Real Self and experiencing all of its feelings. One might call this defense dissociating or moving into a kind of "false observer self" since its awareness is clouded. It is unfocused, as it "spaces" or "numbs out," often out of fear. It denies and distorts our True Self and is often judgmental. By contrast, our True Observer Self has a clearer awareness, observes more accurately and tends to be accepting. Table 9 outlines these differences.

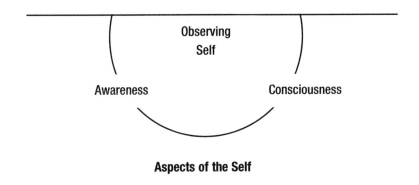

Aspects of the Self

Thinking, Planning, Solving, Worrying

Feeling, Emotion, Affect

Behavior, Action, Functioning

Desire, Wish, Fantasy

**Figure 4. Relationship of the Observing Self
and the Self** (compiled from Deikman, 1982)

Expanding our consciousness, we can soon become aware
of our part in the larger drama—the "cosmic drama." By
watching our own personal dance or melodrama, we can
begin to learn that our Observer Self is that part of us which,
when we realize we are really carrying on (when we *can* realize it), can step back and observe the carrying on through the
power of our imagination. By doing so, we often bring into
play the powerful defense of humor, e.g., by laughing at ourself for taking it all so seriously.

Table 9. Some Differences Between the True Observer Self and the False Observer Self

	True	False
Awareness	Clearer	Clouded
Focus	Observes	"Spaces out" or "numbs out"
Feelings	Observes accurately	Denies
Attitude	Accepting	Judgmental

As our observer self becomes more prominent, our attachment to our false self tends to recede. Primary identification with the false self tends to be associated with suffering and illness. However, building a strong and flexible True Self, which is part of healing our Child Within (in Stage Two recovery), is usually required before we can transition into our observer self for any lasting duration.

REALIZING SERENITY

As we become more familiar with being our observer self and with the healing power of spirituality, we can begin to construct a possible path to realizing serenity, inner peace and happiness. I have condensed the following description from *Spirituality in Recovery* (unpublished), where each is discussed in more detail.

SOME POSSIBLE PATHS TO SERENITY

While we are ignorant of our Journey and therefore limited (humility), we can study universal spiritual laws, approximate them and surrender to our lack of ultimate knowledge.

We are here living out a Divine Mystery. Given these limitations, sages over the centuries describe something like the following:

1. Higher Power is in each of us, and we are in Higher Power. We are an important part of Higher Power, but are not Its totality.
2. We can view our reality and experience as occurring along a hierarchy of levels of awareness, consciousness or being (e.g., physical, mental, emotional and spiritual).
3. We are going Home. (Actually we are Home, already and always.) Home on this Earth is being all levels of our awareness or consciousness in our own unique fashion.
4. There will be conflict going Home (our melodrama or cosmic drama). This conflict or creative tension is useful to us in some way, probably as a way Home.
5. We have a choice. We can use our body, false self and our relationships on this Earth to reinforce our separation and our suffering. Or we can use them as vehicles for our Soul, Spirit and Higher Self to return Home and to celebrate that return.
6. Higher Power (Home) is Love. (Love is perhaps the most useful way we know Higher Power.)
7. We can remove the blocks to realizing our Higher Power by experiencing (including living in the now), remembering, letting go and surrendering. (These four realizations can be viewed as being ultimately the same.) Regular spiritual practice and humility help us with this realization.
8. Separation, suffering and evil are the absence of realizing Love, and are, therefore, ultimately illusions. They are also manifestations of our searching for Love, Wholeness and Home. The evil or darkness is thus ultimately used in the service of the Light.

9. We create our own story by our beliefs, thoughts and actions. What we think and feel in our mind and heart, we will produce in our experience and our life. What we give, we get. As within, so without.

10. Life is a Process, Force or Flow that lives us. We do not live it. When we surrender to it, i.e., flow with its Process and take responsibility for our participation in it, we become co-creators. We can then become free of our suffering that comes with our attachment to resisting flowing with our Life.

11. Inner peace or serenity is knowing, practicing and being all of the above. We ultimately discover that we are already and always Serenity and Home.

Some of these principles are illustrated in the following case history of James, a 42-year-old man who grew up in an alcoholic family, his father being an actively drinking alcoholic and his mother usually assuming the role of a placating co-dependent. While he showed no manifestations of being alcoholic himself throughout his adult life, James was progressively aware of his inordinate confusion and suffering. He eventually attended Al-Anon and later, ACoA self-help group meetings, for a total of about six years, with some improvement. He describes the importance and meaning of the spiritual part of his recovery as follows:

> I went to a lot of Al-Anon and then ACoA self-help meetings over the years, probably one or two a week. I really wanted to get well but didn't seem to be doing it, although something seemed to keep me motivated to keep attending. I had always thought it was important for me to be strong, which I equated with being independent. This meant to me not to talk much. I believed I could recover on my own, without anyone's help. I equated weakness with trusting, surrendering or being dependent, all of which I saw as being a kind of sickness. I viewed people with these characteristics as being sick.

And, of course, I felt I was healthier or somehow better than they were. Looking back I see all of this as a probably necessary defense that allowed me to keep attending the meetings without being too overwhelmed by my hidden feelings and the changes I needed to make to recover.

During that time, I met a woman at the meetings who was really arrogant and unhappy. She was so obnoxious to me that I tried to avoid being around the meetings she attended. I thought there was no hope for her and that I was certainly better than she was. Then I saw her change. She started to lose her arrogant attitude and became friendlier to me and to others. She seemed happy. While I hated to admit it, since it was coming from one who I had never admired, I felt envious of her positive change. I wanted some of that. But she was also now talking about her Higher Power, and I have always had trouble knowing what that was, even though I had had a fairly active religious upbringing.

I began considering what had happened to her and how I might get some of that peace or happiness. It began to occupy a lot of my thoughts and feelings. I'd been through forty years of unhappiness and confusion. I began to read some spiritual literature, and I began to pray. While I had tried to pray since I was a child, there was something different about my praying this time. Perhaps I was more sincere and humble.

Then, some months later, I experienced a kind of transformation that came over about a two-week period. My own attitude changed, and I let go of much of my resentment of my father and of others. (Of course, I had done a lot of work in the past on my anger and other feelings, as well as other of my ACoA issues.) I began to really believe in a Higher Power, something I'd never been able to do. I had first reframed health as peace and happiness and then reframed those as being associated with needing others and God, and surrendering to them and to a spiritual program. Doing so has made all the difference.

James's story illustrates several of the principles of ways to realize serenity (including from the previous list). First, he experienced conflict and struggle (principle 4). He used this struggle in his uncomfortable relationship with the woman he resented as a vehicle for his spiritual evolution and growth (5). He was aware of his conflict and pain, and he began a regular spiritual practice—prayer (7). He eventually asked for what he wanted, this time with sincerity and humility (9), and he surrendered to the process of his life (10). Ultimately he found what he was seeking, and it was inside himself and nowhere else (11).

The traditional or conventional views of attaining serenity or inner peace usually use one or both of either seeking pleasure or avoiding pain. In the *seeking pleasure* approach, the ways of seeking happiness may span a range from hedonistic seeking to focusing on others (which can result in active co-dependence to "being good" and waiting to claim our peace later as a reward in Heaven). In the *avoiding pain* approach we may try to ignore pain, detach from it or stay away from any situation that might bring on conflict. We may ask ourself, *Has either seeking or avoiding ever brought us lasting peace or serenity?* When I have asked this of others and of myself, the answer is usually no.

In response, one of our choices is to feel hurt and resentful about our inability to be happy and to project our pain onto others. Or as an alternative, we might begin to observe the whole process and the self-contraction of our false self when we are unhappy. As we do so, we can begin to see that peace and serenity are not something that we attain. Rather, they are our natural state. Beneath all of what we add to our painful feelings and experience, beneath our self-contraction, lies serenity itself. To realize serenity there is nothing that we need to do or even that we can do. If we make "all A's" on our report card, that won't do it. Neither will owning three Rolls-Royces, nor will having a million dollars or marrying a "Ms. or Mr. Right." There is no way we can earn or achieve peace and serenity, and neither is there any way that we can deserve them. Rather, they are ours inherently, already and always.

For adult children of trauma, accepting this idea that we are inherently at peace and serene may be difficult. If that is so, I think I can understand. As we reach the advanced stages of healing our Child Within, this realization that we are already and always at peace becomes easier and easier. I have found that doing a daily spiritual practice, such as meditation or prayer, and regular reading of spiritual literature have been helpful in realizing my own serenity.

Some readers may be skeptical about this concept of "spirituality." Some may be confused. Others may not believe any of it and may even think, *This author sure has lost it now!* By contrast, others may find some solace in reading it, and still others may identify a lot of useful material here. Whatever your response, I invite you to follow your reactions and instincts. Reflect upon it, talk about it with safe people whenever you may sense that it is appropriate. Use what you can, and leave the rest. Spirituality has worked for me and I have seen it work for hundreds of others in the recovery process.

THE CORE OF OUR BEING IS LOVE

A final way to describe the relationship between the recovery processes and our inherent serenity is shown in Figure 5. As we look beneath the numbness, pain and confusion of our lives that occurred before recovery in Stage One, we can begin to peel away the layers of the onion that have so constricted our Real Self. In healing, we are being like our own sculptor, chipping away at a large chunk of stone until we find the already and always perfect work of art at its center. We slowly work through the fear, shame and anger of Stage Two recovery, and at Stage Three we discover the core of our being: Love.

While God is a Divine Mystery, if God is Love (1 John 4:8),

and if God made us in Its image, and we are each a child of God, then we each are also a spark of that Love. God is also creative and if the above statements are true, then we must each be creative also. *A Course in Miracles* says that God's will for us is that we *be creative* and that we experience complete *peace* and *joy*. Is any of this possible for you? In the space below or in your journal or elsewhere, write anything that may be coming up for you.

_____

_____

_____

_____

_____

_____

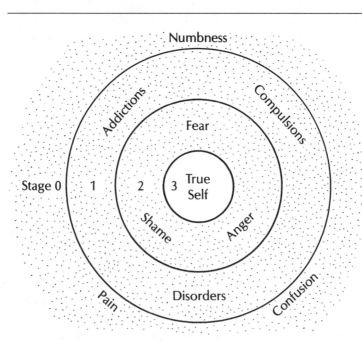

Figure 5. The Constricting Layers of Trauma Effects

As we do the long work of peeling away the constricting layers of self-contraction, of what being attached to our false self has brought us, we can slowly begin to discover that the core of our being is Love. This Love is not infatuation or romantic love, but a mature, peaceful and lasting love. It comes from God and is a part of God. And it is creative.

Would you be interested in opening yourself to feeling this Love right now? It is at the center of your being from which it radiates. It is also all around you, as God's loving energy, and has been called by various names, including Prana, Chi or Ki, Divine Energy and the Holy Spirit.

I believe that this Love is the core of our being. In a search for our True Self, during the recovery process, we peel away the layers of our attachment to our false self. In Stage Three recovery we may eventually discover that the core of our being is creative, Unconditional Love (Figure 6).

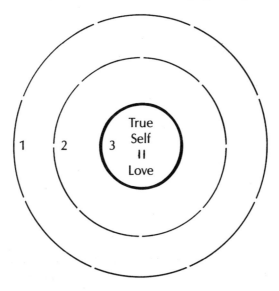

Figure 6. The Core of Our Being Is Love

As you open to your Love, which is also God's Love, would you also consider making a personal recovery plan for developing and deepening your spirituality? If you may be finding it difficult to feel this Love, would you be interested in feeling it?

BEGINNING MY RECOVERY PLAN

To write down a recovery plan for Stage Three, we can first list all of our problems, issues, concerns or blocks that we might have right now. Below are some examples.

- Active addiction lingering (such as nicotine, caffeine, other drugs, sugar, food, work, etc.)
- Incomplete Stage Two recovery
- No regular spiritual practice
- Difficulty experiencing serenity
- Some other problem or concern

Use the space below or elsewhere to write any of your own problems, issues, concerns or blocks.

_____

_____

_____

_____

_____

_____

_____

Given these above problems, what do you want to happen now? For each of your problems, issues, concerns or blocks that you have written above, write in the space on the same page specifically what you would like to happen.

_____

_____

_____

_____

_____

_____

Having written your problems and goals above, you are now two-thirds of the way to completing your recovery plan. To complete it, consider your answer to a final question:

Given what I want to happen regarding each of my problems, concerns, issues or blocks, specifically *how can I accomplish* what I want to happen?

This may be more difficult to answer. Feel free to ask a safe and trusted person, your best friend or your therapist, counselor or therapy group. You may also ask your clergy.* Use the space below to write a draft of your specific plan.

_____

_____

_____

_____

_____

_____

---

*Caution: While most clergy will be helpful, some may be bound up in their own religious beliefs so strongly that they may not understand exactly what an expanded spirituality actually is. If they are fundamentalist in their orientation, you may wish to be cautious here, since they may try to shame or guilt you about your expanding spirituality, and some may even try to convince you that this is the work of the devil. Listen to your clergy— or to anyone from whom you may seek help—only if it feels as if they are nourishing you spiritually. When in doubt, ask other safe people.

The Recovery Plan for Stage Three

Having written the above, you are now ready to write out your formal recovery plan. To assist you in this process, I have written some sample plans below. You may borrow from any of them or use your own ideas, as well as any suggestions from other people that may be helpful.

Sample Recovery Plan for Stage Three

Problem or Condition	What I Want to Happen (Goals)	How I Plan to Reach These Goals
Active addiction lingering	Recover from it so that it won't block my spirituality.	Full recovery program for the addiction (fill in the details here). If necessary, see My Recovery Plan for Stage One.
Incomplete Stage Two recovery	Heal my True Self, including any unfinished business.	Recovery program to address these goals. If necessary, see My Recovery Plan for Stage Two.
No regular spiritual practice	Use a regular spiritual practice.	Select a spiritual practice. Practice it daily. If necessary, learn it from a teacher.
Difficulty experiencing serenity	Experience serenity.	Continue regular spiritual practice, as above. Let go of fear and other pain. Open to experiencing the Love that is within me.

On the next page is a blank form where you can write out your own recovery plan.

MY RECOVERY PLAN FOR STAGE THREE

Name (optional) _____ Date _____

Problem or Condition	What I Want to Happen (Goals)	How I Plan to Reach These Goals

CORE ISSUES IN SPIRITUALITY

In reading various holy books and working with spirituality over the years, I have found sixteen core issues in the area of spirituality (Table 8). We can consider using any of these core issues in making our recovery plan, just as we may have in our recovery plan, for Stages One and Two recovery.

CO-CREATING OUR LIFE

Another way to assist us in reaching the goals we have written in our recovery plan is to explore using the process of co-creation, which is a kind of spiritual practice.

Our healing journey takes us from co-dependence—living from our attachment to our false self—to co-creation, creating what happens to us and how we feel in concert with our Higher Power. It is a long, sometimes difficult journey, but one that may be worth taking.

When we let our false self run our life, we are numb or hurting, often afraid, ashamed and empty. If we get stuck in this state, and our True Self remains in hiding, we can become nearly immobilized. No matter what may be happening on the surface or how we may try to handle it, we are usually hurting. We feel separated and alienated from our True Self and from our Higher Power, and we cannot create anything. Do we have to stay this way? Is there any way out?

The only way to ease our pain, to fill our emptiness and experience any lasting peace is to realize our True Self, then experientially connect it to God. That is the essence of the co-creation process.

What is God's will for me? While we each have to discover what God's will is for us in our own way and in our own time, working a spiritual program helps most people in their

Table 8. Core Issues in Stage Three (Spirituality) Recovery and Living

Core Issue	Early	Middle	Late
Trust	Sorting	Learning	Letting God
Ego attachment	Recognizing ego	Releasing ego	Being real
Being authentic; honest	Learning inner life	Awareness of God within	Being real
Patience (living in the Now)	Learning to handle frustration	Observing and experiencing	Being in the Now (holy instant)
Accepting paradox	Recognizing paradox	Practicing acceptance	Clear vision; Christ's vision
Openness; humility	Willing	Learning	Attitude of being "nobody special"
Tolerance	Learning not to judge others	Practicing not judging others	Being non-judgmental
Gentleness	Learning tolerance	Practicing it & . . .	"
Groundedness	Realizing potential	Practicing it & . . .	Being grounded
Peacefulness	Wonder, awe	Gratitude	Joy, abundance
Defenselessness	Willing, letting go	Innocence	Defenseless
Communion	Prayer*	Meditation*	Conscious contact
Giving, generous	Learning to give** in order . . .	to keep, all things . . .	That are of God
Miracle minded	Aware of choice	Choose God	Let God do the rest
Forgiving	Practice miracles	Let go toxic beliefs***	"
Faith	Learning to trust God . . .	. . . to help us in many problems	. . . in all problems
Self-realization	Going within to find we have a choice****	Find we are a crucial part of God	Being God's Child, innocent and safe

*These two may be interchangeable.
**The opposite of the world's definition.
***Belief in separation, sin, guilt/shame, fear & death.
****Choice for God—see text of *A Course in Miracles*.

143

recovery. And while it all remains a Divine Mystery, some holy books have discussed God's will. The clearest discussion of God's will that I have found is from *A Course in Miracles*. It says that God's will for us is that we have complete peace and joy, and that we be creative.

I believe that once we have healed our Child Within and thereby realized our True Self, and when we have begun to connect experientially to God, we have already begun the process of co-creation.

THE PROCESS OF CO-CREATION

Figure 7 shows a map of the process of co-creation. The first half of the process, shown on the left side of the figure, is what *we* do. It is our work. And the remaining half is what we *surrender* and *let God* do.

NAME THE FEELING, DYNAMIC OR ISSUE

It is important to become fully *aware* of what is coming up for us from moment to moment in our inner life and then, if useful, to give it an *accurate name*. When we heal our trauma effects, we will be tuned in and fully aware of our inner life, thus able to know what it is that we are experiencing. We can give an accurate name to anything in that inner life: any belief, thought, feeling, want, need, intuition, pattern or anything else.

For example, we can name ourself as an Adult Child of a dysfunctional or troubled family. Or a trauma survivor. I remember how enlightening and empowering that was for me when I realized and accepted that fact for myself. Did anything like that ever happen to you?

Another example is when I feel angry, and feel it fully. Doing so tells me several things—that I may have been

144

mistreated or have lost something important and that I may need to set some healthy boundaries or take some other action, or that I have misperceived a conflict.

EXPERIENCE MY INNER LIFE

Before we can work through any of our pain, we have to both name it and experience it. To experience something, we open ourselves and allow whatever might be in our inner life right now to come up into our awareness. We usually cannot name something unless we can *experience* it. And when we name it, that helps us experience it more accurately and completely. These feed one another in a positive reciprocation.

As we experience our inner life, we will learn that some of our pain is necessary—for example, when we grieve a loss.

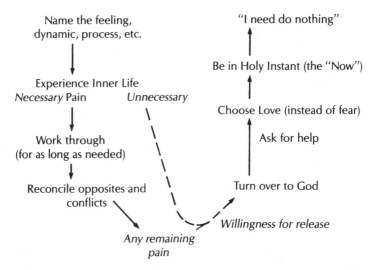

Figure 7. Some Steps in the Process of Co-Creation

145

We also learn that some of our pain is not necessary. We don't actually need to experience it. For example, when we beat ourself up for getting a parking ticket. In reality, being upset for longer than about five minutes is usually unnecessary in that kind of situation.

WORK THROUGH THE PAIN

As we experience necessary suffering, we begin to work through it. And as we work through it, we experience it more accurately and completely. This shows how the process of experiencing, naming and working through it can act together in a healthy way as we work through the pain or upset. And it is work. It takes a lot of energy, grief and time to do this work and complete it.

We cannot rush our grief work, our necessary pain.

RECONCILE OPPOSITES AND CONFLICTS

Part of our work will eventually involve beginning to iden-tify, sort out and reconcile conflicts on which we are working. For instance, do I stay in this relationship or leave it? Do I stay with this job or go elsewhere? Should I risk being real or con-tinue not to be? Yes or no? Or somewhere in between?

Once we have identified the opposites, one of the first core issues that we can work through is all-or-none. To stay in the all-or-none mode is to be rigid and constricted. Being flexible releases and empowers us. Remember that in work-ing through any all-or-none conflict, we usually have more choices. So for each conflict, we ask ourself, *What are my choices?* I may not need to choose "all" (stay in this relation-ship, job or be false) or "none" (leave, work elsewhere or always be real with everyone). In fact, I might be able to do something in between. So I consider what I want to do, share it with safe others and take plenty of time to work it through.

ANY REMAINING PAIN

Having done our part of the co-creation process, we can now more strongly involve our Higher Power. This does not mean that we don't have to stay in conscious contact with the God of our understanding from the beginning or during working through our upset, issue or concern. Doing that is certainly appropriate, useful and empowering.

TURN IT OVER AND LET IT GO

Now we are ready to assess how much, if any, pain may be remaining. How much do we still hurt? When we sense that we have done all that we can do for now, we can take any remaining pain and turn it over to our Higher Power. We let go of it. We let it go.

But to do this, to let go, we must be willing. The Big Book of AA and its equivalents in other Twelve-Step fellowships speak of the importance of being willing to let go and to change. *A Course in Miracles* talks repeatedly of the healing power of just "a little willingness." All we need, then, is to be willing to have any remaining pain removed. The Course says that taking away our pain is precisely one of the major jobs of the Holy Spirit. It takes the pain, outshines it, and it is gone.

And so, being willing to have our pain removed, we ask that the Holy Spirit remove it. And then we let it go. It can feel like stepping off a cliff and trusting that we will not be hurt. We don't know what form the change or help might take, but we have faith that our Higher Power will guide and nurture us in exactly the way that we need.

If we feel stuck in any way, we can assess whether we have

done all we can do to work through our conflict. If there is more for us to do, we can do it, then let go of any remaining pain. And throughout this entire process, we can ask our Higher Power for help.

When we have done all our work, and when we let go of any remaining pain, we can actually feel the pain lifted from us. It disappears. It is gone.

CHOOSE LOVE

Just as we let go of the pain, we can now choose Love. Many holy books describe Unconditional Love as the most powerful, creative and healing energy in the universe. And so we choose to experience it, to have it flood our body, mind and spirit. We experience Love in our Total Being.

Thus when we experientially choose Love, we are pure Serenity, complete peace and joy, which is God's will for us. The Course calls it the Holy Instant, others called it Nirvana and Christ called it the Kingdom of Heaven. It is all the same state of pure Unconditional Love.

Have you ever walked into a room that was pitch black, completely dark, and searched for the light switch—and finally turned on the light? When you flipped the switch, what happened to the darkness? It probably completely disappeared. That is what happens when we choose Love over fear or any other pain. The pain simply disappears. The light outshines the dark.

I NEED DO NOTHING

We are now in complete peace and joy. We are in the Holy Instant. What do we need to do then? The Course says that we can remember just four words: "I need do nothing." There is no more for us to do. All we need to do now is to just be.

In this state of peace and joy, we are the most creative and empowered that we can ever be. We have allowed the healing and creative Unconditional Love of our Higher Power to come into and permeate our being. We have discovered the core of our being: Unconditional Love. (See Figure 6.)

THE FEAR OF TRANSCENDENCE AND LOVE

When we feel that serenity, when we feel the Love that is within us, we may also feel scared. We may feel that if we let ourself feel good, even joyful, that something bad will happen. And so, by attaching to our false self, we constrict and contract from feeling that Love.

We may do this because in the past when we did feel good, something bad did happen to us or someone else. What we may not have known was that at that time we did not feel authentically good from our True Self. We were not then consciously connected to our Higher Power. We may have been rather grandiose or inflated in our ego, false or co-dependent self. Our ego attachment may have led us to feel that we were separated from others and from God. At times we may have even felt that rather than being a part of God, a Child of God, that we were the totality of God. We can call that state or feeling *ego inflation.*

EGO INFLATION

At times, trauma survivors can feel inflated, thus inauthentically powerful or good in several ways. Jungian author Edward Edinger has described at least seven factors that might bring out ego inflation. These include:

- Acting like an adolescent, which he and others have called the *puer aeternus* (eternal adolescent). This can

149

happen to many people with active co-dependence, addictions and other disorders.

- Inappropriate outbursts of false pride or attacking others.
- Motivation for power and omnipotence. Playing God.
- Playing martyr or victim, and its exaggeration, playing tragic hero or heroine.
- Manipulating, that is, trying to get something indirectly.
- Being narcissistic in an unhealthy way.
- Not paying attention to our unconscious, including any unfinished business that we may have.

I have noticed two more such factors:

- Trying to avoid experiencing and working through necessary pain.
- Basking in self-pity or unnecessary pain.

Caution: Be careful of the trap of seeing everyone else's pain as unnecessary and all of yours as necessary.

One way to guard against becoming inflated is to practice being its opposite: being humble. *Humility* is that state of being open to experiencing and learning about self, others and God. In this openness we are free not only to avoid any of these above factors when possible, but we are also free to connect with our Higher Power.

In this state of humility and innocence, we can experience whatever comes up for us, which may be joy or pain. And we can then just be in that joy or work through the pain, whatever that pain is due to.

When we are not our True Self, innocent and humble, and when we do not experientially include God in our life, we can end up trying to live from our ego or false self, feeling separated and alienated, feeling empty and without meaning.

TO ENJOY FEELING GOOD

How can we enjoy feeling good? Consider doing the following: When we feel good, excited, happy or expansive and no factors for ego inflation are present, and we are in conscious, experiential contact with our Higher Power, we can then simply let ourselves feel good. And it is likely that nothing "bad" will happen. Daily spiritual practice, such as prayer, meditation and reading spiritual literature, can facilitate this process.

You may want to consider taking the following self-assessment survey about your spirituality. There are no right or wrong answers.

I wish you the best on your journey in Stage Three recovery.

Spirituality Self-Assessment Survey

Please make a check mark, circle or underline about where you feel you are in the following areas:

1. I live in the Here and Now.
Never   Seldom   Occasionally   Often   Usually

2. I know there is a Power greater than myself.
Never   Seldom   Occasionally   Often   Usually

3. I turn the negative things in my life into the positive.
Never   Seldom   Occasionally   Often   Usually

4. I regularly practice some form of meditation or prayer.
Never   Seldom   Occasionally   Often   Usually

5. I feel open to learning about myself from others.
Never   Seldom   Occasionally   Often   Usually

6. I exercise regularly.
Never   Seldom   Occasionally   Often   Usually

7. I am able to detach from my frustrations by viewing my life as a "game" or melodrama.
Never   Seldom   Occasionally   Often   Usually

8. I am amused about or laugh at myself.
Never   Seldom   Occasionally   Often   Usually

9. I am able to concentrate or focus on what I am doing.
Never   Seldom   Occasionally   Often   Usually

10. I accept "what is."

Never   Seldom   Occasionally   Often   Usually

11. I regularly take time off for myself for relaxation and recreation.

Never   Seldom   Occasionally   Often   Usually

12. I see the paradoxes in my life, i.e., life's opposites, as compatible with each other.

Never   Seldom   Occasionally   Often   Usually

13. I regularly work a self-help program (e.g., AA, Al Anon, other).

Never   Seldom   Occasionally   Often   Usually

14. Even though I do not always get what I want, I see everything that happens to me as having a purpose.

Never   Seldom   Occasionally   Often   Usually

15. I love someone and feel loved by someone important to me.

Never   Seldom   Occasionally   Often   Usually

16. I have a sense of being able to differentiate my false self (or ego) from my True Self.

Never   Seldom   Occasionally   Often   Usually

17. Regarding my death, I feel prepared and mostly unafraid.

Never   Seldom   Occasionally   Often   Usually

18. I feel an emptiness or void.

Never   Seldom   Occasionally   Often   Usually

19. I have a meaning, purpose or mission in my life.
Never   Seldom   Occasionally   Often   Usually

20. I am honest with others.
Never   Seldom   Occasionally   Often   Usually

21. I am honest with myself.
Never   Seldom   Occasionally   Often   Usually

22. I practice letting go of unnecessary pain.
Never   Seldom   Occasionally   Often   Usually

23. I feel unconditional love for another.
Never   Seldom   Occasionally   Often   Usually

24. I choose to have peace of mind.
Never   Seldom   Occasionally   Often   Usually

25. I feel connected to others and to a Higher Power.
Never   Seldom   Occasionally   Often   Usually

26. I feel sexually fulfilled.
Never   Seldom   Occasionally   Often   Usually

27. I trust most people.
Never   Seldom   Occasionally   Often   Usually

28. I am gentle.
Never   Seldom   Occasionally   Often   Usually

29. I enjoy even my most menial tasks, such as cleaning the
    toilet.
Never   Seldom   Occasionally   Often   Usually

30. I accept others' choices for themselves, even when they differ from what I would choose for them.

Never   Seldom   Occasionally   Often   Usually

31. I feel firmly balanced and grounded.

Never   Seldom   Occasionally   Often   Usually

32. I feel accepting and accepted.

Never   Seldom   Occasionally   Often   Usually

33. I feel unconditionally loved.

Never   Seldom   Occasionally   Often   Usually

34. I am aware of my feelings as they come up for me and I handle them in a healthy way.

Never   Seldom   Occasionally   Often   Usually

35. Other (please write in)

_____

_____

_____

_____

_____

_____

_____

_____

_____

_____

_____

There are no right or wrong answers to these items.

(This survey has been researched by Corrington, Killoran and others.)

REFERENCES

Anda RF, Croft JB, Felitti VJ, Nordenberg D, Giles WH, Williamson DF, et al. Adverse childhood experiences and smoking during adolescence and adulthood. *JAMA.* 1999; 282:1652–1658.

Alcoholics Anonymous: The Basic Text for Alcoholics Anonymous [the "Big Book" of AA]. Third edition, Alcoholics Anonymous World Services, New York, 1976.

Anonymous (1976). *A Course in Miracles.* Foundation for Inner Peace/Viking, New York.

Anonymous: *The Urantia Book.* Urantia Foundation, Chicago, 1955.

Anonymous: *A Course in Miracles.* Foundation for Inner Peace, Box 635, Tiburon, CA 94920,1955.

Barker, L.R. and Whitfield, C.L.: Alcoholism (chapter 21) in Barker, L.R. et al. (eds.) *Principles of Ambulatory Medicine.* Third Edition, Williams & Wilkins, Baltimore, MD 1991.

Corrington J: Spirituality and recovery: relationships between levels of spirituality, contentment and stress during recovery from alcoholism in AA. *Alcoholism Treatment Quarterly* 6:151165,1989.

Deikman A: *The Observing Self.* Beacon Press, Boston, 1982.

Dietz PM, Spitz AM, Anda RF, McMahon PM, Santelli JS, et al. Unintended pregnancy among adult women exposed to abuse or household dysfunction during their childhood. *JAMA*. 1999; 282:1359–1364.

Edinger E: *Ego and Archetype*. Penguin Books, Baltimore, 1973.

Felitti VJ, Anda RF, Nordenberg D, Williamson DF, Spitz AM, Edwards V, Koss MP, et al JS. The relationship of adult health status to childhood abuse and household dysfunction. *Am J Prev Med*. 1998; 14:245–258.

Finkelhor D, Hotaling G, Lewis IA, Smith C. Sexual abuse in a national survey of adult men and women: prevalence, characteristics, and risk factors. Child Abuse Negl. 1990; 14:19–28.

Gorski, T. and and Miller, M.: *Counseling for Relapse Prevention*, Herald House: 1982.

Hazelden. *Hope and Recovery: The Workbook*, CompCare Pubns., 1994.

Hecker LL, Whitfield CL 2000. Advice and Adage: Interview with Charles L. Whitfield, M.D. on the psychotherapy of childhood trauma survivors, *Journal of Clinical Activities, Assignments & Handouts in Psychotherapy Practice*. Volume I (3):95–103.

Jones, K.R. and Merchant, S., et al: *Core Issues in Early Recovery*, outline from the Resource Group, Baltimore, MD 1986.

Kendler KS, Karkowski LM, Prescott CA: Causal relationship between stressful life events and the onset of major depression. *American Journal of Psychiatry* 156: 837–841, 1999.

Kendler KS, Bulik CM, Silberg J, Hettema JM, John Myers J, Prescott CA: Childhood Sexual Abuse and Adult Psychiatric and Substance Use Disorders in Women: An Epidemiological and Cotwin Control Analysis. *Arch Gen Psychiatry*. 2000; 57:953–959.

Killoran CA: A spiritual dimension of gestalt therapy (doctoral research project through UMI), Ann Arbor, MI, May 1993.

Kurtz E: Not-God: A history of Alcoholics Anonymous. Hazelden Educational Services, Center City, MN, 1979.

Lash J: *The Seeker's Handbook: The complete guide to spiritual pathfinding.* Harmony Books, NY, 1990.

Lazaris: *The Crisis of Martyrhood.* Concept Synergy, 302 S. County Rd, Ste. 109, Palm Beach, FL 33480 (407-588-9599)

Lukoff D, Lu F, Turner R: Psychoreligious and psychospiritual problems. *Journal of Nervous and Mental Diseases* 180:11, pages 673–682, 1992.

Lukoff D, Turner R, Lu S: Transpersonal psychology research review: psychospiritual dimensions of healing. *Journal of Transpersonal Psychology* vol 25:2,1993.

MacMillan HL, Fleming JE, Trocme N, et al. Prevalence of child physical and sexual abuse in the community: results from the Ontario Health Supplement. *JAMA.* 1997; 278:131–135.

May G: *Simply Sane.* Paulist Press, NY, 1977.

Middelton-Moz, Jane, & Dwinell, Lorie: *After the Tears: Reclaiming the Personal Losses of Childhood,* Health Communications, Deerfield Beach, FL, 1986.

Moore T: *Care of the Soul.* HarperCollins, NY, 1992.

Nouwen H: *Life of the Beloved:* Spiritual living in a secular world. Crossroad, NY, 1992.

Pagels E: *The Gnostic Gospels.* Vintage/Random House, NY, 1979.

Pam A: A critique of the scientific status of biological psychiatry. *Acta Psychiatrica Scandinavica* 82:1–35 (Supp l362), 1990.

Pam A: Chapter 1. Biological psychiatry: science or pseudo-science? In Ross CA & Pam A: *Pseudoscience in Biological Psychiatry*. John Wiley, NY 1995.

Ring K: 1992: *The Omega Project* William Morrow, New York, NY.

Rodegast P, Stanton J: *Emmanuel's Book II: The choice for Love*. Bantam, NY, 1989.

Ross CA & Pam A: *Pseudoscience in Biological Psychiatry*. John Wiley, NY 1995.

Ross CA: Chapter 2. Errors of logic in biological psychiatry. In Ross CA & Pam A: *Pseudoscience in Biological Psychiatry*. John Wiley, NY 1995.

Ross CA: Chapter 3. Pseudoscience in *The American Journal of Psychiatry*. In Ross CA & Pam A: *Pseudoscience in Biological Psychiatry*. John Wiley, NY 1995.

Vallenstein *Beyond the Brain*, Basic Books, NY,1998.

White Eagle: *The Quiet Mind*. White Eagle Publishing Trust, New Lands, Hampshire, England, 1972.

Whitfield, Charles, L.: "Co-dependence: Our Most Common Addiction—Some Physical, Mental, Emotional and Spiritual Perspectives," *Alcoholism Treatment Quarterly*, 6:1, NY, NY 1989.

A Gift to Myself, Health Communications, Deerfield Beach, FL 1990.

Whitfield CL: *Boundaries and Relationships*, Health Communications, Deerfield Beach, FL 1993. (. . . also translated and published in French and Spanish editions)

Healing the Child Within, Health Communications, Pompano Beach, FL 1987.

Co-dependence, Health Communications, Deerfield Beach, FL 1991.

Spirituality and Recovery, Perrin & Traggett, Rutherford, NJ (1-800-321-7912): 1985.

Wisdom to Know the Difference: Transforming Co-dependence into Healthy Relationships.

Whitfield CL: Adverse childhood experience and trauma (editorial). *American Journal of Preventive Medicine,* 14(4):361–364, May 1998.

Whitfield CL: *Memory and Abuse,* Health Communications, Deerfield Beach, FL 1995.

Whitfield CL: *The Truth about Depression,* Health Communications, Deerfield Beach, FL 2003.

Whitfield CL: *The Truth about Mental Illness,* Health Communications, Deerfield Beach, FL 2003.

Whitfield CL: *Boundaries and Relationships,* Health Communications, Deerfield Beach, FL 1993.

Whitfield CL: *The Spiritual Psychology of Jesus Christ: What He Really Taught and Continues to Teach.*

Wilber K: *No Boundary.* Shambhala, Boulder, CO 1978.

Writings of the third Zen patriarch (Sengtsan): *Hsin Hsin Ming —verses on the faith mind.* Universal Publications, 2512 Haven Rd., Virginia Beach, VA 23452.

ABOUT THE AUTHOR

Charles L. Whitfield, M.D., is a physician and psychotherapist in private practice in Atlanta, Georgia. He is a nationally known speaker and the author of *Memory and Abuse, Boundaries and Relationships* and the national bestsellers *Healing the Child Within* and *A Gift to Myself.* His two most recent books include *The Truth about Depression* and *The Truth about Mental Illness.*